RESILIENCE

STORIES AND LESSONS FROM
AN ARDENT PHOTOGRAPHER

RESILIENCE

ISBN: 978-0-578-80830-7

Book cover art and interior design by Stone Ridge Books LLC.

RESILIENCE

STORIES AND LESSONS FROM
AN ARDENT PHOTOGRAPHER

Ron B. Wilson

To Renzo,

for showing me how to be resilient

TABLE OF CONTENTS

FOREWARD

BY DANIELLE DA SILVA

Founder & CEO

Photographers Without Borders

I founded Photographers Without Borders in 2009, before social media had truly taken hold. The world was changing, as it always does. There was a new president of the United States, the first Black man to fill the office. The obsession with the "War on Terror" was subsiding. As the daughter of a Muslim Indian parent, it was an important moment. It felt like I could be myself again. I felt optimistic. And I wanted to be of service.

For decades and centuries, the symptoms of colonialism have presented themselves in many ways—poverty, environmental degradation, famine, social justice. These postcolonial effects take on many forms in the Global South. What the Global North, or "Western" world, sees as problems inherent to these nations (that they happen to be suited to fix), communities around the world see as problems caused by the West that *they* now have to fix. Back in 2009, the rest of the world was just starting to open its eyes and see the bigger picture. Photographers Without Borders seeks to serve those communities by leveling the playing field and amplifying little-heard voices with storytelling.

Ron has been one of our greatest advocates over the years. He has traveled all over the world with us on multiple assignments, and we have grown together as a result. In this book, you will be taken on some of these adventures, but more importantly, you will hear the voices of resilience in ways that I hope will open your mind and lift your heart.

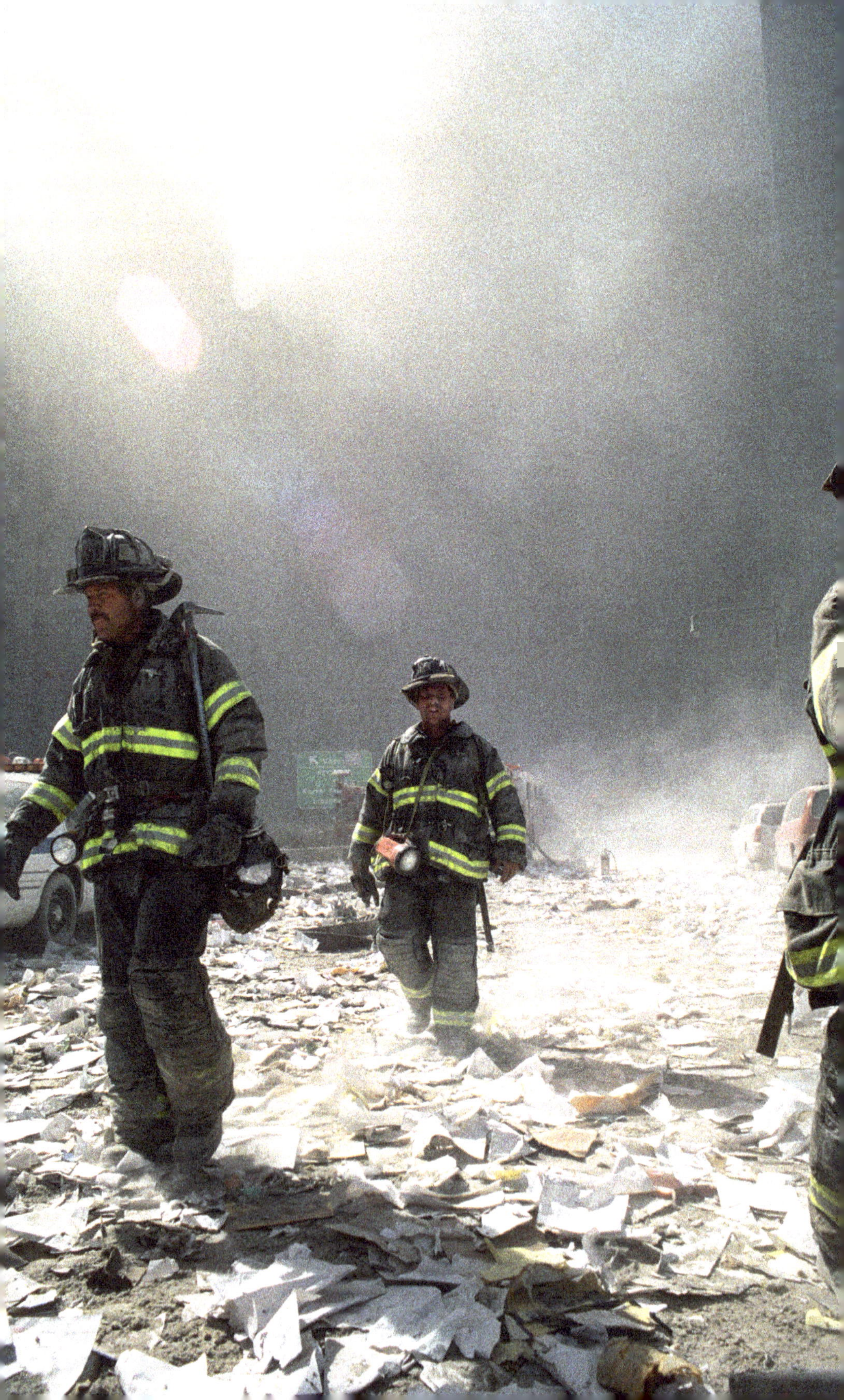

CHAPTER 1

THE DAY THE WORLD CHANGED

"When times get tough, we don't give up. We get up."

– President Barack Obama

Just before 9 a.m. on September 11, 2001, I got a phone call from my friend Lilly, a photojournalist working for the *Miami Herald*. She told me there was a small plane crash at the World Trade Center, near my place, and wondered if I could go downtown to shoot some photos. We both interned for the *Herald* years ago, and if nothing else, she figured, I could get published in the paper.

I quickly got up, grabbed my gear, film and batteries, and ran out the door.

I lived on 23rd Street in New York City, near a subway stop. Leaving my apartment, I walked into a splendid September day: low humidity, abundant sunshine. It was a Tuesday, primary day for the upcoming municipal elections, which would decide the successor of Rudy Giuliani. Later that day, the polls would close early and end up being postponed for two weeks.

I jumped on the downtown 6 Train, anxiously wondering what was happening. All the other riders were already talking about "the accident" in ominous voices and hushed tones, an air of mystery wafting throughout the crammed train.

I made it to Canal Street before the entire train line stopped. The conductor's voice crackled over the intercom, informing us that trains were no longer traveling southbound. Our journey was over. We needed to get off.

By the time I peeked above ground, having climbed what seemed like endless stairs ascending into the streets of lower Manhattan, I already knew this was no accident.

I TAKE THE RESPONSIBILITY of this story very seriously. To be part of it, even in the smallest way, was my destiny—the most consequential day of my life. A switch had been flipped for me. There was my life before 9/11, and my life afterwards. I believe I was chosen to be in New York on that day, to contribute in any way possible. And in return, it would change who I was for the rest of my life.

Even though I grew up in rural Florida, I believe my presence in the city on this pivotal day was no coincidence. My great-grandparents immigrated to the U.S. from Germany before the First World War, arriving, like thousands of others, at Ellis Island. They settled in Staten Island. As a kid growing up in the balmy south, my grandmother, Augusta Corbitt—Gram, I'd call her—would tell me stories about New York City, the bright lights and chaotic lifeblood seeming like a whole other country. She loved to talk about the 1964 World's Fair, a shining moment of American pride before the Vietnam War rocked the nation. She voraciously read every copy of *National Geographic* and kept all her back issues stacked on her screened-in porch, where I'd spend whole days thumbing through them with the heavy floral smell of jasmine flowers in the air. Those years cultivated my passion for travel, a passion that would one day, years later, take me back to the Big Apple with dreams of becoming a professional photographer.

I remember the first time I saw the Twin Towers in 1986, working a brief gig at a family friend's restaurant on Long Island. They were a North Star for us lost souls—always there, guiding us, so tall they seemed to ascend forever, especially at night. In fact, when they were first built in 1972, they were literally the tallest buildings on Earth, surpassing the mighty Empire State Building. They were arguably the most famous structures in the world. Instantly recognizable. Symbols of America. A landmark to the strength of technology when matched with breathtaking ambition.

For me, the one word that describes that day, and the 20 years since, is "resilience." It describes the emergency personnel, the city itself and its residents, as well as my life and career. It defines me. It defines the city I love.

No, I don't believe I was in New York by accident on that day. Everything I had done in my life—all the experiences I had, the people I met, my years of academic study—they had brought me to that moment on the crammed subway staircase, trudging upward along hundreds of my fellow New Yorkers.

I WORMED MY WAY out of the concrete stairwell onto an asphalt landing, looking south. By this time, both buildings had been hit; black smoke and fire billowed out.

I knew immediately this was no accident. I remember thinking this would be the worst day in history—at least my history. But when I first saw the destruction, my initial thought was naive: *Oh; the firemen are here. They'll go up and put out the fire.*

Fire trucks and sirens were racing in every direction.

It'll be okay, I figured.

But as I moved closer, walking past terrified people running in the opposite direction or simply paralyzed with fear, I realized the extent of my shock and denial. I sensed the horror and astonishment on everyone's face. I remember noticing New York's diversity in this moment: people of every nationality were suddenly speaking the same language, and you could understand them perfectly by looking at their faces.

And then, as I was still weaving through the streets of Lower

Manhattan, the South Tower fell. It took just a few seconds to disappear completely.

Once I emerged onto the West Side Highway, I finally got a clear view of the carnage. Was there really only one tower? It was unbelievable. I'd seen these buildings as immovable since the 1980s, as simple facts of life, part of a landscape that doesn't shrink, but always grows. You don't imagine looking out your window one day to discover a mountain suddenly missing.

There were so many rumors on the street that day. Cellphone service was cut, so I wasn't able to contact anyone. People across the world watching on TV knew more than us on the ground. We were left to our imaginations, scrambling amid the stories spreading among us. Was it an accident? Was it on purpose? Was it terrorism? Were the planes hijacked? What's that about an explosion at the Pentagon? Were people really jumping from the buildings? If so many people thought the better option was to jump, I can't even fathom how horrible it must have been to be trapped inside that inferno.

Manhattan was on lockdown. Anything seemed possible. But I kept moving south, as the bad got worse.

I DON'T KNOW HOW TO explain this, but I see the numbers "911" everywhere. Pretty much every morning, as if even my circadian rhythm is traumatized, I somehow glance at my watch at 9:11. Sometimes at stores or restaurants, my receipt is for purchases worth $9.11. It's on a license plate, in someone's phone number. All the way in Lima, Peru, I even found myself sleeping in room 911 at the Westin Hotel.

It follows me, and I believe the reason is to remind me—remind me to be here, today, writing this, keeping this story alive.

When I say my life changed after September 11, 2001, I mean that literally. I developed a bad case of asthma and severe allergies, things I never suffered from while growing up. I started drinking heavily to handle the trauma, to suppress memories that haunted me. I sabotaged a relationship and fell so far behind on my taxes that the government started garnishing my wages. I was depressed and morose, symptoms I now can recognize as belonging to post-traumatic stress disorder.

Still, I was fortunate. I was able to pull myself together. I got my asthma under control with inhalers I still use every day. I got my career back on track. I met someone in 2002, and we've now been married since 2015. September 11 damaged me, but it didn't destroy me. New York rebounded in the same way. That's what I mean by resilience.

Rather than make this story about me, I want to be perfectly clear: I didn't take these photos for myself, or even for the *Herald*. While thousands of lives were lost that day, countless more were saved by the heroism of the city's first responders. I am writing this for them—especially those who died in their virtuous struggle. I witnessed firsthand all the unbelievable work these true American heroes did that day, sacrificing everything to help save the lives of strangers.

That day, New York City's bravest rose to their biggest challenge. Faced with the worst, they gave us their best. I ran toward the burning buildings alongside them while others ran away, but make no mistake: I am not the hero of this story. They are. I merely witnessed this moment, helped document it so the details could never be disputed or forgotten. The best way to honor these heroes is to show them at their best.

AT 10:28 A.M., THE SECOND ground-shaking roar began. This time, I was much closer. I knew there was nothing I could personally do to help, but my instincts took over and I kept shooting. By this point, along with everything and everyone else, I was covered in a thick, hellish white powder. God only knows what I inhaled that day. The air was thick with dust and debris, airplane fuel and human remains, sharp bits of metal and loose sheets of paper; it was impossible for us on the ground to avoid the medley of toxic fumes washing over us. I scrambled to cover my face and camera at the worst times, but could only cover so much. My asthma is my lifelong memento.

I remember hearing a police officer yell into his two-way radio, "It's gone. The World Trade Center is gone." Paramedics and firefighters ran everywhere with emergency equipment and empty stretchers. But there was no one to save—everything was gone.

Once under that cloud, unable to see anything else, all I could think was that the rest of downtown must be gone too. That it was all destroyed. The anxiety of not knowing was overwhelming. There were massive fires everywhere; cars were exploding. I wasn't sure I'd survive. It truly was like a war zone.

Amazingly, these same first responders kept returning to Ground Zero day after day, week after week, month after month. They still knew they needed to help search for survivors. Meanwhile, staff at the local hospitals waited for new patients that would never come.

I remember how much I loved being downtown and looking up, seeing that proud skyline marked by two untouchable rectangles. Once the dust cleared a bit, I was able to look up and see for the first time, clearly, that they had simply vanished. They had disappeared, like a perverse magic trick. I stood there in absolute disbelief.

The world had truly changed.

As I ran out of film and headed home, I reflected on the valor and inspiration I witnessed. Firefighters ran into rubble. Police officers saved lives. Strangers hugged on the street. Store owners gave away bottles of water to people in need. That's the true story of 9/11: the story of resilience.

I WANT TO CONTINUE telling this story for the generations who won't remember this momentous event, or those who weren't even born yet. I was an observer of history. That's why, 20 years later, I'm finally realizing my dream of commemorating the event with a documentary film. Our goal is to find the subjects of my photographs and their families and interview them about their lives before, during and after that fateful day. My colleague and I want to better understand the ramifications, on a human scale, of this global disaster.

I believe that in life, in every experience, you should take away as many lessons as you can—and always try to leave a little of yourself behind. We grow while helping others grow. We survive by sharing our stories, our knowledge and our memories. This is the ripple effect that's essential to humanity's existence, and especially our heroes, whose work never ends.

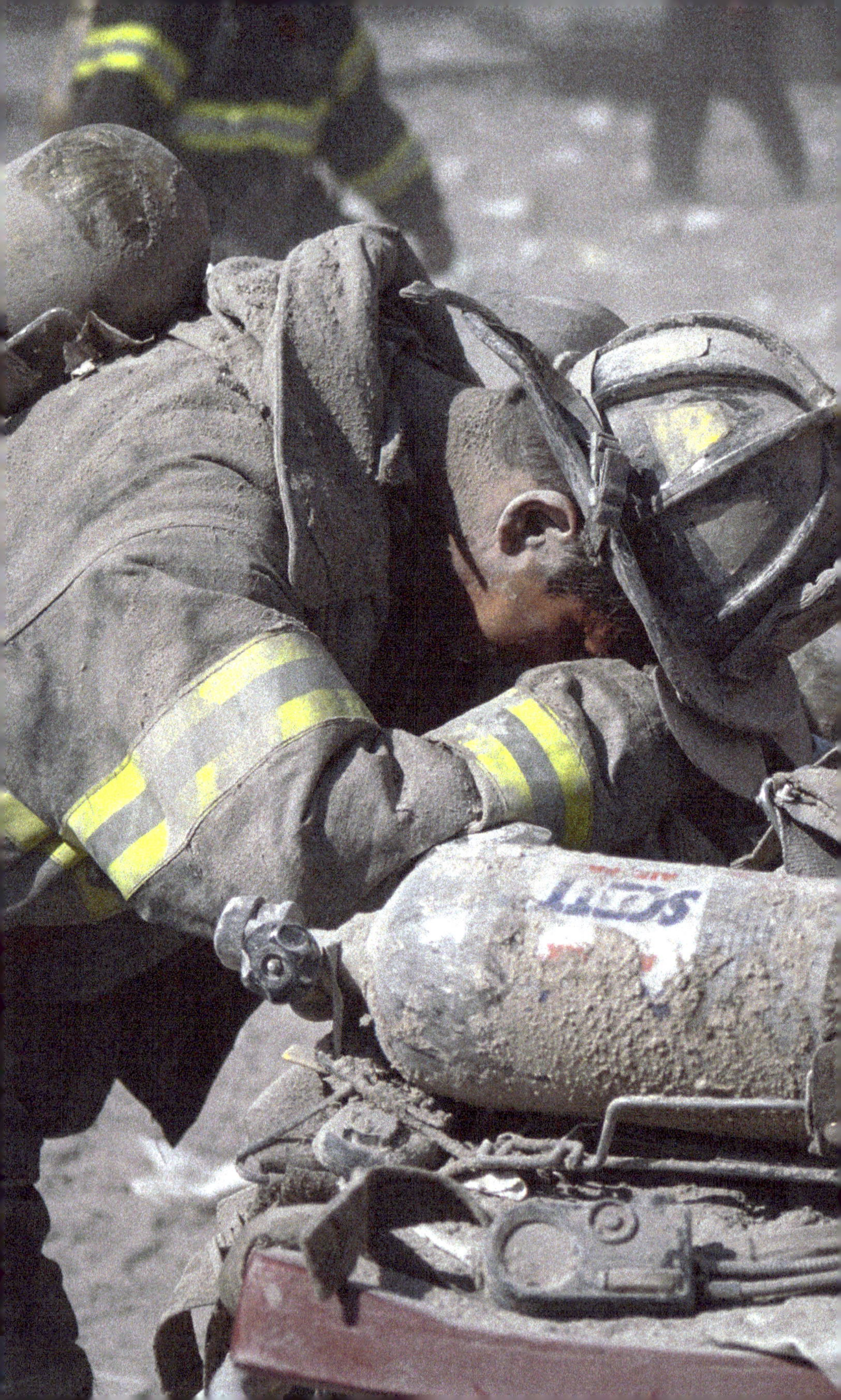

A PHOTOGRAPHER'S LESSON FROM 9/11

I've been asked a few times before: how did I keep my camera clean on 9/11? It was a challenge for sure. In truth, I don't remember all of it—that day is like a hazy memory to me now. I recall stopping in my tracks to cover my face and camera at moments when the dust became unbearable. I always carry a microfiber cloth with me—I probably used that. But even looking back at those original negatives today, some look grainy and hazy. Maybe they're just old negatives, or maybe my lens just wasn't as clean as it could have been. In a moment like that, a little grit on your lens becomes part of the story.

THROUGHOUT THIS BOOK, I'd like to share some tips on photography and travel I've accumulated over the years. I want you, the reader, to be able to take something tangible away from all this. You've already given me the gift of your time by reading my book—I'd like to return the favor and offer something in return.

So in between these chapters, to break up the stories, I'm going to offer short bits of wisdom I've learned over the years. These tips will tackle the art and business of photography, from basics for beginners to lessons I've learned from decades as a professional. If you're an aspiring photographer, or even just a hobbyist, I hope you'll find some of this insightful. If you're familiar with the basics, you may find some of it redundant; then again, you may learn something unexpected.

And if you're not a photographer at all, you may still appreciate the life lessons that come from photography. Like other art forms, I find cameras to be a great metaphor for the human condition. They are complex machines that require patience and care. They are constantly evolving; and their observations can change the world.

So while I can't speak with 100 percent accuracy as to how I kept my camera clean during 9/11, I'd nonetheless like to share a few tips on keeping your gear as neat and safe as possible. Even a single grain of sand can ruin an SLR lens, so it's important to protect your investment.

1. **Avoid changing lenses out in the open.** This is especially true if you're in a dusty or sandy area, like a beach. You can't risk sand or water getting inside the camera sensor or rear area of the lens. I also never set my gear down directly on the ground—only inside my bag.
2. **Avoid changing lenses by preparing your bodies in advance.** As a follow-up to that first point, I typically carry two camera

bodies equipped with different lenses—for example, a 24-70mm and a 70-200mm. That would offer me a wide range of options, so I don't have to switch lenses at all. I also keep some UV filters attached more or less constantly to some lenses, which double as protective shields, in addition to regulating the light. Scratching a $70 filter would suck, but not as much as scratching a $2,000 lens.

3. **Always clean your gear immediately after a shoot.** I'm meticulous about putting away my equipment after it's been cleaned. Otherwise, you're contaminating your camera bags with dust and whatever else might have gotten on your camera. The added benefit of this is having 100 percent working, clean gear available at a moment's notice.
4. **Have everything serviced often.** This is my most important recommendation. I suggest having your equipment cleaned and maintained every six months or so. It only costs around $100 (a small fraction of what new gear would cost), and it makes it much easier to avoid problems and save me the hassle of Photoshopping out dust spots.

Finally, I'd like to leave you with a broader thought: just as it's critical to keep your camera clean, you should also keep your body and mind clean. Bodies are not so different from cameras: we both need routine maintenance to ensure our complex systems continue to work well. And the good news? Rarely is it too late to start.

This is a lesson I take very personally. I mentioned a period after 9/11 when I wasn't taking care of myself. But after those dark days, I got back on my feet, dove deep into health and wellness, and am now proud to live life as someone who puts care and effort into not just myself, but those I interact with, as well. When I talk about resilience, that's what I mean. You can always start taking care of yourself, being mindful of your body and using that positivity to be a force for good in the world.

It's a lesson I didn't fully appreciate when I was younger. But now that I'm older, I wish I could go back in time and give myself some advice.

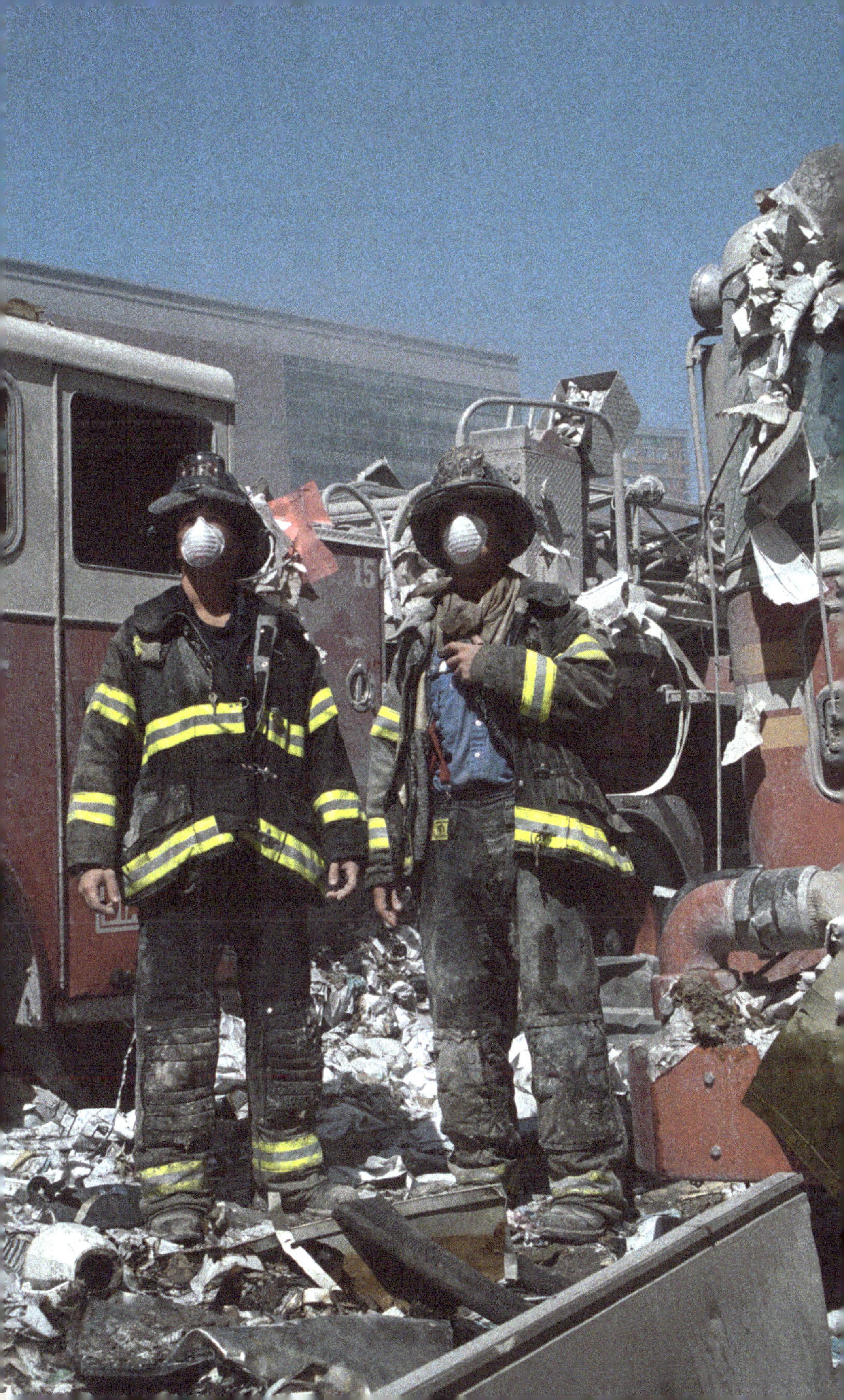

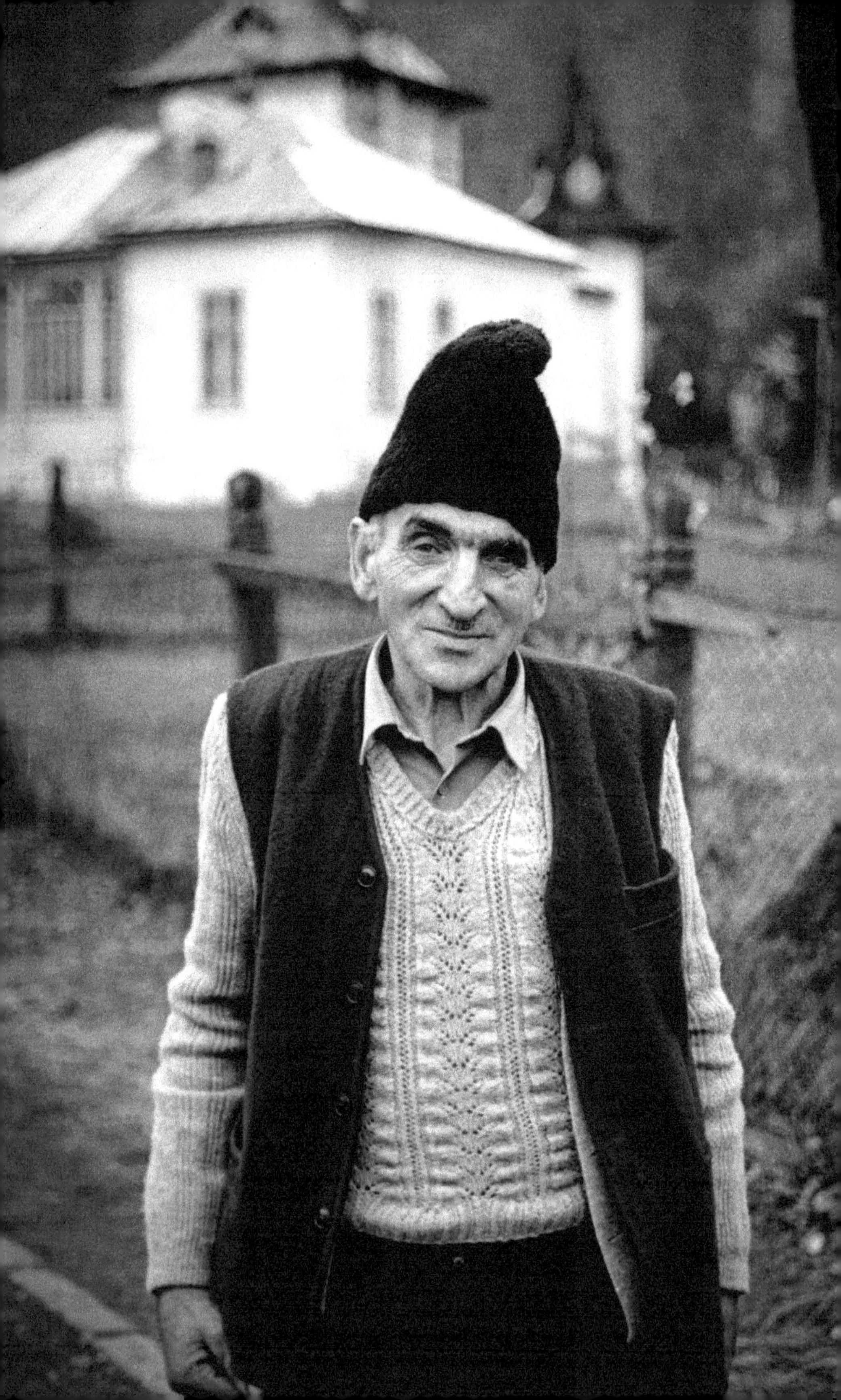

CHAPTER 2

BACK WHEN IT ALL BEGAN

"The photograph reflects, every streetlight a reminder/ Nightswimming deserves a quiet night."

– Michael Stipe, R.E.M.

In late 1992, I rented a car with little more than the desire to see the world outside my small hometown in North Florida. Not sure where I was going, or why, I teared up when I said goodbye to my parents and tried to explain how I wanted to follow my passion for photography by hitting the road alone.

"Aren't there things in Florida to photograph?" asked my mom, Nancy.

There were, of course. But there was much more to see in the rest of the country.

Before I left, my decision didn't make sense to anyone—including me. I was young and antsy, unencumbered by debts, family commitments or material possessions. I was light-footed and free. At the time, it was merely a feeling I wanted to explore, a self-inflicted rite of passage. Looking back, it wasn't even a choice—it was something I had to do.

I headed west. I didn't bring much, just a new (second-hand) Minolta XG-1, some rolls of color and black-and-white film, a Sony Walkman and my three favorite cassette tapes: Marky Mark and the Funky Bunch's *Music for the People*, Madonna's *Erotica* and *Automatic for the People* by R.E.M. I had a few thousand dollars to my name that I'd saved up from about six months of bartending, but aside from that, all I had was a newfound thirst for travel.

Along the way to California, I saw so much of the country during what felt like pivotal years of a new, modern decade. I drove across Bourbon Street in New Orleans. Just like Paul Simon predicted, I was received in Graceland; I passed a "Welcome to Arkansas" sign; I picked up a hitchhiker en route to the Grand Canyon. Spirited by music, I made it to Amarillo by morning and got my kicks on Route 66. After all that, I landed face-first on a friend's couch in Venice Beach, California, where I crashed for a while.

I was hooked on travel. I felt rejuvenated by my total freedom and blissful solitude, and I took advantage of every moment possible to snap away at foreign sights. My camera was my icebreaker: an all-in-one tool to introduce myself to strangers, document natural wonders, dissect architectural designs and study people's faces.

Having sort of settled in California after all these adventures,

I was hungry for more. It was time for round 2. I spent a short stint as a morning-shift manager at a beachside bakery in L.A., after which I felt nervous calling my mom to tell her I'd bought a one-way ticket to Amsterdam. What would she say? She fretted over my driving to a different coast; now I was crossing an ocean.

As it happened, I didn't have much to worry about. When I was growing up, she always advised me to do whatever made me happy. She saw that photography was my road to happiness. Over the phone, her assurance that she'd love me no matter what I decided, whether I had a plan or not, was fuel enough to spark the fire in me then—and continues to inspire me today.

So I flew to Amsterdam. But I didn't end up staying there: I ventured off to Germany, Czechoslovakia, Hungary, Romania, Bulgaria, Turkey, Israel and Egypt, meeting fascinating people and taking lots of bang-up photos along the way. After months of traveling, I made it all the way past Abu Simbel to the border between Egypt and Sudan before I ran out of money.

Those final days of my trip—floating down the Nile on a felucca with some fellow travelers; experiencing rural life on the African continent; observing the brilliant dancing stars every night, unwilling to sleep; laughing, living and listening to the songs I'd learned every word to—those were some of the best times of my life. They shaped me into the person I am today.

AFTER I GOT BACK HOME, I showed my friends and family my photographs. Everyone was very supportive, and more than a few people encouraged me to hone my skills at photography school. Buoyed by their faith in me, I enrolled in a two-year photography program at the Art Institute of Fort Lauderdale in October 1993.

Digital cameras were still a few years away, so all my classes centered around film SLRs, different photographic genres and manual settings. I took classes in applied photography, design, black-and-white and color darkroom printing, and the history of photography. I learned about studio lighting, portraiture, photojournalism, fashion, commercial and product photography. This education cast a wide net that helped me understand the industry and where my skills fit in.

Some people scoff at art school, preferring to jump into the creative world immediately and claiming that art can't be taught. While I understand where they're coming from, personally, I find myself still today reflecting on much of what I learned during those two years, and the department introduced me to a community of peers whose friendship was invaluable.

During my first semester at the art institute, we went over some photography basics. Even though I knew much of what they were teaching us, having experimented for several months on my trips across the United States and Europe, I still appreciated learning the rules in a formal way. Like the old saying goes, you have to know the rules before you can break them. By the end of my two years there, I ended up graduating with an admirable GPA and winning the coveted "Best Portfolio" award in my graduating class.

Before graduating, however, I was selected for an internship at the *Miami Herald.* This turned into a critical experience that helped mold me into the person I am today. I photographed everything for them: breaking news, portraits and daily features. After graduating and finishing my internship, I stayed in touch with the photo desk at the *Herald* as a freelancer and moved to Budapest for another internship with the Atlantic News Service. My assignments were truly world-class. Europe in the 1990s was undergoing an incredible transformation: communism had collapsed, globalism was ramping up and fighting in the Balkans would determine what the continental map looked like for decades to come. I ended up covering Hilary Rodham Clinton's visit to Eastern Europe and traveled to Sarajevo to see the aftermath of the Bosnian War.

After returning to the United States, I eventually relocated to New York City to fulfill my dream. I bounced around, shooting whatever I could in a variety of industries, building my portfolio and a name for myself. It wasn't until 9/11 that everything collapsed—and not until a few years later that I decided to rebuild my life into the kind I wanted to live.

WE COMPLICATE OUR LIVES with "things." As we age and acquire more, it's easy to lose sight of what matters. But really, life comprises split-second moments that will never be repeated. I'm energized by not knowing what's around the next corner; it's chasing light and searching for something or someone to photograph. For me, this isn't the stuff that happens only on weekends or vacations, when we can get away from life. This *is* life.

Nothing makes me happier than being in an unfamiliar place with my gear, ready to get to work. Documenting what I see, starting a day where everything is new—I do it mostly for myself. It's icing on the cake when people enjoy my work and are willing to pay me for it, especially if I can help tell someone else's story along the way.

I've seen and experienced many things since that life-defining trip 25 years ago. I like to share my feelings with complete strangers and laugh in many languages. A quarter-century later, I helped document 9/11, accessed the remnants of the Chernobyl nuclear power plant, snapped photos of wild animals on a South African safari and worked with non-profit organizations in India, Guatemala, Guyana and Botswana, in between trips to Morocco, Peru and Cuba that have blended the personal with professional. These are the stories you'll read about in this book.

I still have those albums by Marky Mark, Madonna and R.E.M. The only difference? Now they're on my iPhone. I like keeping them as tunes of inspiration for those difficult moments. If I ever get cynical, my go-to song is “Nightswimming” by R.E.M. As soon as those jangly piano keys kick in, I’m immediately transported back to the banks of the Nile, where I can smell the heat and dry sand, taste the swirl of Arab spices and feel the seductive dance of the stars overhead.

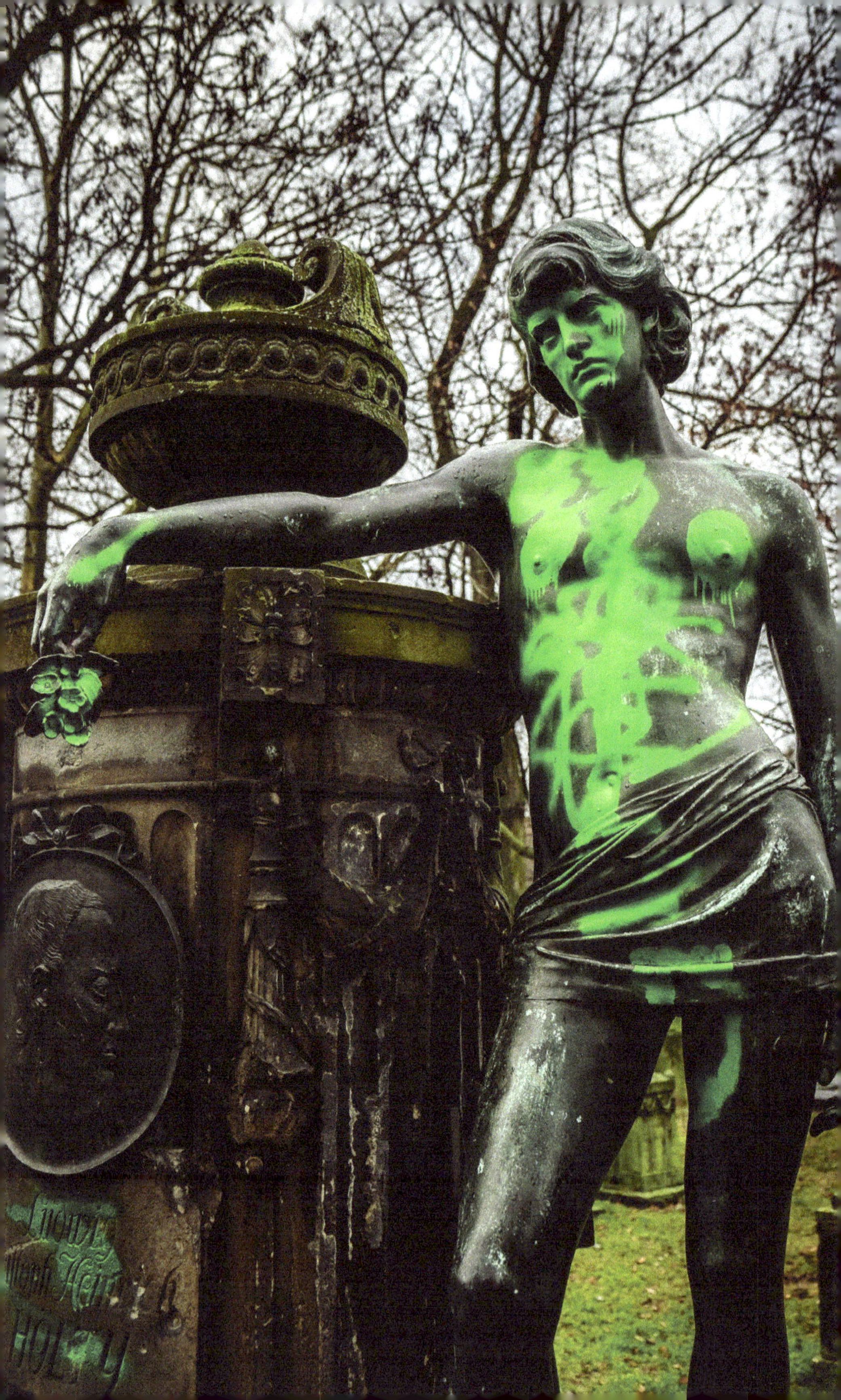

PHOTO TIP: FINDING CREATIVITY

Creativity is one of the most important things in the world. That's not just true for artists and photographers: learning how to think creatively will almost certainly benefit you in any career, from finance to construction to medicine to cutting hair. Creativity and critical thinking go hand in hand. It's a way to solve problems and understand concepts in a new light. And, like most things, it can be learned.

I'd like to offer a few tips on how I get my own creative juices flowing. These tips are meant primarily to help photographers, but really, anyone reading this can pick up something useful.

1. **Try new things.** Strive for originality. Find your voice. Use everything at your disposal to create fresh images you love. It's not just about gadgets; it's about improvisation. Use a car's sun shade as a reflector or a small fan to blow a subject's hair. Get silly. Get your subject to be silly, too—it makes every photo shoot more fun. By trying new things and looking at the world through your unique eyes, you can build a body of work to be proud of.

2. **Have a personal project.** As a photographer, you will of course take on assignments to pay the bills. You may not love every project. That's normal. But by keeping a personal project going at all times, you can give yourself a creative outlet to continue exploring your passion. This is also great because it keeps photography from becoming strictly business—once that happens, it's no fun at all. Plus, it gives you a project to discuss with clients and friends, which can drive your career forward. Personally, projects like my "Men in Hats" series (images of men in different headgear around the world) isn't something I'm shooting for money, but it's still something I frequently talk about and plan on slowly building over the years.
3. **Let others inspire you.** When I'm in a rut—and we've all been there—the best way for me to get inspired is to browse my favorite photographers on Instagram. No, I'm not trying to steal anything; photo streams like Instagram, Pinterest and Flickr are just awesome for mood boards that burst with inspiration. This can apply to anything, beyond even photography—you can get easily inspired for your next vacation or passion project online. When I find something I like, I study it: what kind of lighting did the artist use? Why does the composition work? And forget photography: you can watch beautifully shot movies and ask the same questions, study the same visual language. Where is the scene set? How does the story unfold? Does it create a

certain mood or atmosphere? Is it realistic? Is it funny? Is it romantic? How does the cinematographer convey that emotion, if you were to strip away the script and soundtrack? Once you make a list of what aesthetics inspire you, take those elements and incorporate them into your next shoot.

4. **Make it personal.** Sometimes a great story or idea comes from your own life. Without a personal connection, it can be tricky to fully commit to a project. I often feel a personal connection to the places I visit, but it's not a coincidence. I *look* for those connections. When I happened to be in Morocco during the anniversary of 9/11, it gave me an opportunity to reflect on the relationship between the United States and the Muslim world. When Photographers Without Borders sent me to Botswana, I thought about all the people I'd known personally who suffered from HIV and AIDS. When I flew to Cuba, I realized how close it had been all my life—just 90 miles from the tip of my home state. Connecting personal ideas and telling personal stories will help you connect with your audience—that's true of photography, writing and public speaking.
5. **Never stop learning**. I've considered myself a photographer for nearly 30 years, and I still recognize that I'm developing my skills. I still find new artists who inspire, challenge and surprise me. It reminds me that I have to keep practicing my craft to stay sharp in the game. Besides, with how fast the industry is

evolving, you have to keep learning. I couldn't keep relying on film once everyone started asking for digital files. And when mirrorless cameras came in vogue, I immediately started researching them and determined they could revolutionize my travel habits—they're much smaller and lighter. Of course, that also meant more research on brands, lenses and trends. Photography is fun like that. Not only are styles and aesthetics constantly changing, but the technology is changing with it.

I hope this inspires you to go out there and create something, regardless of whether or not anyone ever sees it. Do it for yourself. Capture a place in time through your lens. Don't focus too much on the gear and equipment you have; focus on stretching the boundaries of your art. Come up with an idea and hit the ground running. If photography is what you care about, then that's the only thing worth doing.

If you're still feeling stuck, here's a checklist I often run through before starting a project. Tick off each box, and your art will start coming to life before you realize it.

1. Make a list of ideas
2. Research your topics
3. Look at other artists' work or blogs and magazines for inspiration
4. List what equipment you'll need
5. Make a schedule for how much time you can devote every week
6. Define what outcomes or goals you want to achieve with this project
7. Ask yourself, what's the story you want to tell?
8. Interview people in the field you are working in

Finally: just go ahead and create it!

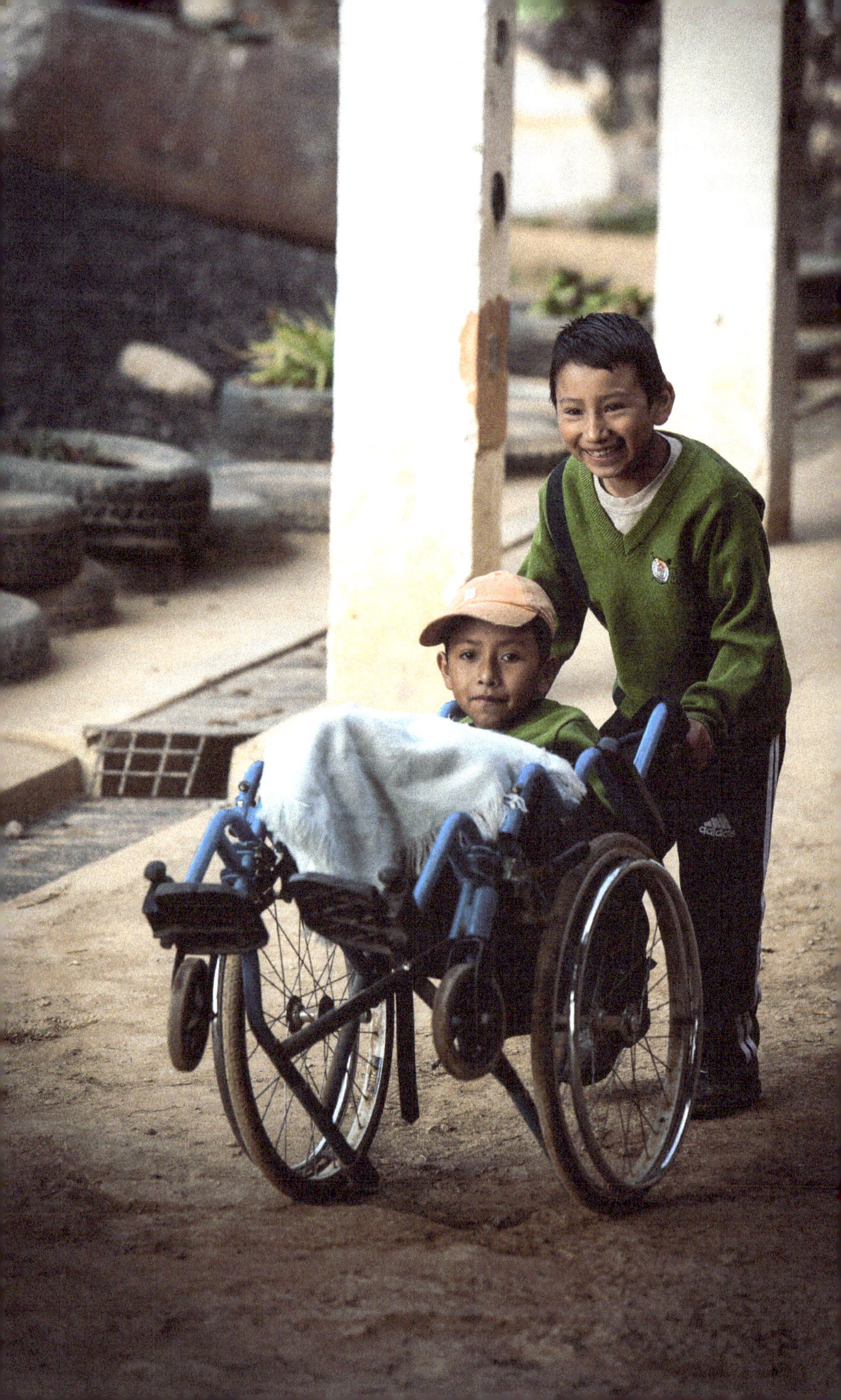
adidas

CHAPTER 3

PASSION IN GUATEMALA

"Cada loco con su tema."
("Everyone is passionate about something.")

– 17th-century Spanish proverb

Glancing at the boy, you could assume a lot about his life. He looks no older than 10. He might be a bit grumpy, confined to life in a wheelchair from a young age. He is lithe and small with a cap that looks a size too big. He's staring dead at you with a blank stare, maybe suspicious—or maybe just falling out of a passing daydream.

When I photographed this boy, though, I didn't see an unhappy kid. I saw a trusting community. Because there's more to the photo than just a kid in a wheelchair. This boy's friend, a schoolmate in a matching forest-green uniform, gripped his wheelchair and thrust it back, popping a wheelie and laughing hard. The boy in the chair isn't bored or thrilled—he just kind of seems used to it. His friend probably does this all the time.

That moment became one of my favorite shots from my trip to

Guatemala, and an emblem of how I would feel about the country as a whole. The atmosphere was rich with faith in the community, comfort among one other, children running freely and fearlessly. They don't constrain themselves with shame and inhibition, the way our North American manners confine us. They lack the cursed privileges that lead many of us to abundance, anxiety and petty first-world problems; these kids, at least in the town I visited, were sincerely grateful just to be in school.

Guatemala marked my first foreign photography assignment in many years, and it rejuvenated me completely. I'd spent the previous two decades mastering the craft in other ways. Having always been fascinated by human stories and emotions, in the mid-2000s, I migrated toward wedding and portrait photography. I spent many lovely years capturing the most important day in people's lives, and I've been lucky to grow my business well enough to be able to pick and choose my projects. I worked leisurely, largely controlling my own schedule and working with clients I genuinely liked.

But every career has its lulls, and by 2015, I became complacent and a little unmotivated. Weddings are special and unique, but when you do so many in a year, they can also become routine. I needed to shake things up. I needed to rediscover my passion. And the only way back, I reasoned, was to reconnect with the spirit of what drew me to photography in the first place: travel.

I'd traveled independently before, with no assignments or contacts, but I knew that wouldn't satisfy my itch. I craved purpose. I wanted to use my camera for good, the way I had on 9/11, by documenting moments of pure emotion, heroism and community. I needed to rediscover the humanity in front of my lens.

So I decided to search for a nonprofit organization that could leverage my technical skills for a worthy cause. Ideally, I wanted to partner with a group that would allow me to travel to less fortunate parts of the world with my gear and document cultures and projects that deserve more awareness than they currently receive.

I didn't need to search very hard. The result came up immediately: Photographers Without Borders.

I quickly read their mission statement and scoped out some of their past projects. Volunteers are sent around the world to document the work of specific partner NGOs and interview the locals, community leaders and volunteers involved. Founded by Danielle Khan Da Silva, PWB is sort of like pro bono marketing for global NGOs that match the organization's high ethical standards, but with a strong emphasis on telling the human stories behind their efforts. It would provide me complete access to resilient people working in difficult circumstances.

Immediately, I felt this was the right match for me. After filling out an application and submitting my portfolio, I was delighted to be accepted as a member. I scoured their open assignments—Sri

Lanka, Cambodia, India—and eventually threw my name in the hat for two countries: Guatemala and Ghana.

It wasn't a straight line to my destination. Over the next couple months, I was accepted to the Ghanaian project, and began quickly planning out all the gear I'd need, ideas for photographs, daily itineraries and local sights. I began researching Ghana's wretched history of slave castles—forts built to essentially jail Africans until they could be sold and shipped abroad—and it fascinated me to learn about a continent whose culture and tragedies I frankly knew little about. But that project got delayed, and I wound up switching to Guatemala because it fit within the same timeline.

I had to pull something of a 180, researching life on an entirely different continent. Ultimately, however, I believe everything ended up for the best, because I actually speak some Spanish, which would come in handy in a small town two hours from Guatemala's capital city. Plus, who wouldn't prefer a three-hour plane ride over a 19-hour slog with two layovers? For a first outing, Guatemala was perfect.

The landlocked town was called San Juan Comalapa, with a population of about 30,000 in the country's south. Its dusty roads, colorful street art and colonial cathedrals are bordered by verdant mountains and clear blue skies. The most famous landmark is easily the Church of San Juan Bautista, widely renowned for its intricate paintings that blend ancient Mayan lore with Christian themes. Inspiration comes easy here, since artistic pride is a theme of the entire town. It's the birthplace of many famous Guatemalan artists, such as the native Kaqchikel painter Andres Curruchiche. For this reason, people today still call Comalapa "the Florence of the Americas."

Here was a rural artistic gem tucked away in the Guatemalan mountains. Comalapa was exactly what I needed to reignite my passion.

My mission would be to document an organization called Long Way Home. They build local schools using sustainable design ideas and recycled building materials, hiring locals to construct and work in the schools.

But before getting there, I needed to raise the project fees associated with the trip—costs for airfare, insurance, vaccinations and donations for my hosts. PWB helped set me up with an online fundraising site, so I could request support from my friends, family and clients. To my surprise, my network flooded my account with money rather quickly, putting my dream within reach.

After reaching my financial goal of about $3,000, the date for my travel was set: February 29, 2016. The next steps were to purchase my plane ticket and other pre-travel items, and finally to make contact with Long Way Home before embarking on my adventure. Once all of my tasks were complete, I was introduced to Genevieve, the project coordinator in Guatemala. I felt immediately drawn to her, with her bright red hair and laid-back vibe; she was clearly professional, genuine and transparently passionate about her work. In fact, she and I ended up becoming close friends, even working together in a whole other industry, years later in Peru.

A year had passed since I initially learned about PWB, six months slipped by after receiving my assignment, two months of pre-departure work had been completed, and then I was finally closing my front door with photo gear and luggage in hand, about to fly to Guatemala.

I READ IN A GUIDEBOOK somewhere, many years ago, that the best way take advantage of traveling is to essentially forget your life back home and give in to your new surroundings. That passage helped me enjoy a rewarding experience in Guatemala.

Of course, the food tasted unfamiliar. People drove differently. My Spanish wasn't exactly fluent. But the sights were breathtaking, and the smells intrigued me endlessly. Having time to notice the small differences in culture, and having the open-mindedness to embrace them, is a fulfilling way to travel.

The work being done by Long Way Home was visually striking, which made my job easy. The NGO was founded in February 2005 by Matt Paneitz, a Texan who's never lost his accent, even after spending all these years in Guatemala speaking Spanish daily. Matt decided to study eco-building in the United States and apply his education south of the border. He's a little scruffy, very laid back and mostly quiet—that is, until you ask him about a subject close to his heart.

Matt and his early team began their mission by building a community park on a five-acre plot of rural land. The green space now boasts an organic garden, soccer field, community kitchen and pavilion, having transformed from a little-used field into a bustling local hub. Today, their mission has expanded to cover more robust projects across the region.

I can't fault Matt for starting his NGO here in Comalapa. I will never forget the city's mesmerizing colors, painted on every wall and stitched into every item of handmade clothing. I will always remember the aromas of the bustling street-side markets that overflowed onto concrete sidewalks. And the art was as inescapable as it was transfixing: I don't often buy physical artwork, but one of the few that still hangs on a wall in my home is by a native artist named Oscar Peren, whose intensely colorful pieces showcase a vibrant, kinetic, sometimes surreal vision of Guatemala. I ended up photographing Oscar in his gallery and meeting his son, Roberto, who was helping construct the school with Long Way Home. This warm sense of community is partly what drew me into Guatemala, and what made it so hard to leave at the end of my time there.

After my assignment, I spent a couple days in Antigua, a larger city (still just 45,000) surrounded by volcanoes and renowned for its Spanish colonial buildings. Most of the structures have been restored after a major earthquake in 1773 ended Antigua's 200-year reign as Guatemala's colonial capital. I stayed with a caring host, Donal, and his amazing family, and captured some amazing images that still fill me with wonder when I look back at them.

But more than anything—the NGO, the cities, the artwork—I will cherish the genuine smiles and jubilant laughter of the children on the campus at Long Way Home. My trip to Comalapa was filled with so many vivid memories, and I only hope that my photographs can adequately represent the sincerity of the people I met, the dedication of the staff and all the hope they deliver every day.

MY TRIP TO GUATEMALA set the tone for my four subsequent adventures with Photographers Without Borders. Not only did Guatemala shake me out of my comfort zone and reinvigorate my love of photography, but it also helped me realize what was important in this world. Community, health, freedom—these matter deeply. But fundamental to all of them is education.

I didn't choose my destinations this way, but education turned out to be a recurring theme in all my assignments with PWB. Maybe it's because the organization works with so many education-focused NGOs, or maybe my instinct pulled me in those directions. I'm not quite sure.

Either way, I've come to appreciate how delicate it is that education should be considered a right, not a privilege—a profoundly human right, as much as freedom and health. This is true in North America, but it's especially important for marginalized people and those in rural communities. Education is a central tenet of smaller communities, binding cultures together under the shared love of their children. Education is optimism: if our children are smarter than us, maybe they'll help solve the problems we couldn't fix.

When I shot family portraits in Guatemala, I noticed the differences between each generation in the frame, and how they stood united by blood despite their obvious differences. The older generations, with wizened faces and blistered hands, spent their lives working in agriculture; the younger ones, slimmer and more intellectual, have yet to discover what paths lie before them.

Education is a key. That key opens the door to whole other worlds: languages, countries, opportunities. "Knowledge is power" is not just a saying; it's the truth.

One of my favorite photographs from Guatemala is of a large, colorful map of the Americas. I noticed a little girl skipping in front of it without a care in the world. I was lucky to press the shutter button at just the right moment, as both her feet flung into the air. I love this image because of the geopolitical context right behind this innocent girl. The map reminds me just how close Guatemala and the United States are. It reminds me that these people are our neighbors and we should think of them as family. In fact, in many Latin American countries, "America" isn't synonymous with the U.S.—it's what you call all the Americas collectively. Literally, we are all Americans.

When we help to uplift communities like these, everyone benefits. That's why I decided to create a non-profit organization that I hope will bring professional photography services, pro bono, to grassroots organizations to help bring awareness to their missions.

A friend recently asked me what my life goals were. I answered truthfully: "To help people help other people."

If I only put serious effort into helping people personally—if I focused on only helping people I could meet face-to-face—I wouldn't be able to help more than a few dozen people over my entire life. But directing my efforts toward organizations that are already helping hundreds or even thousands of people, I'm leveraging my time so much more efficiently. For me, that means casting a wide net, employing my talents for good, spending my time freely and getting out what I put in. The possibilities are endless.

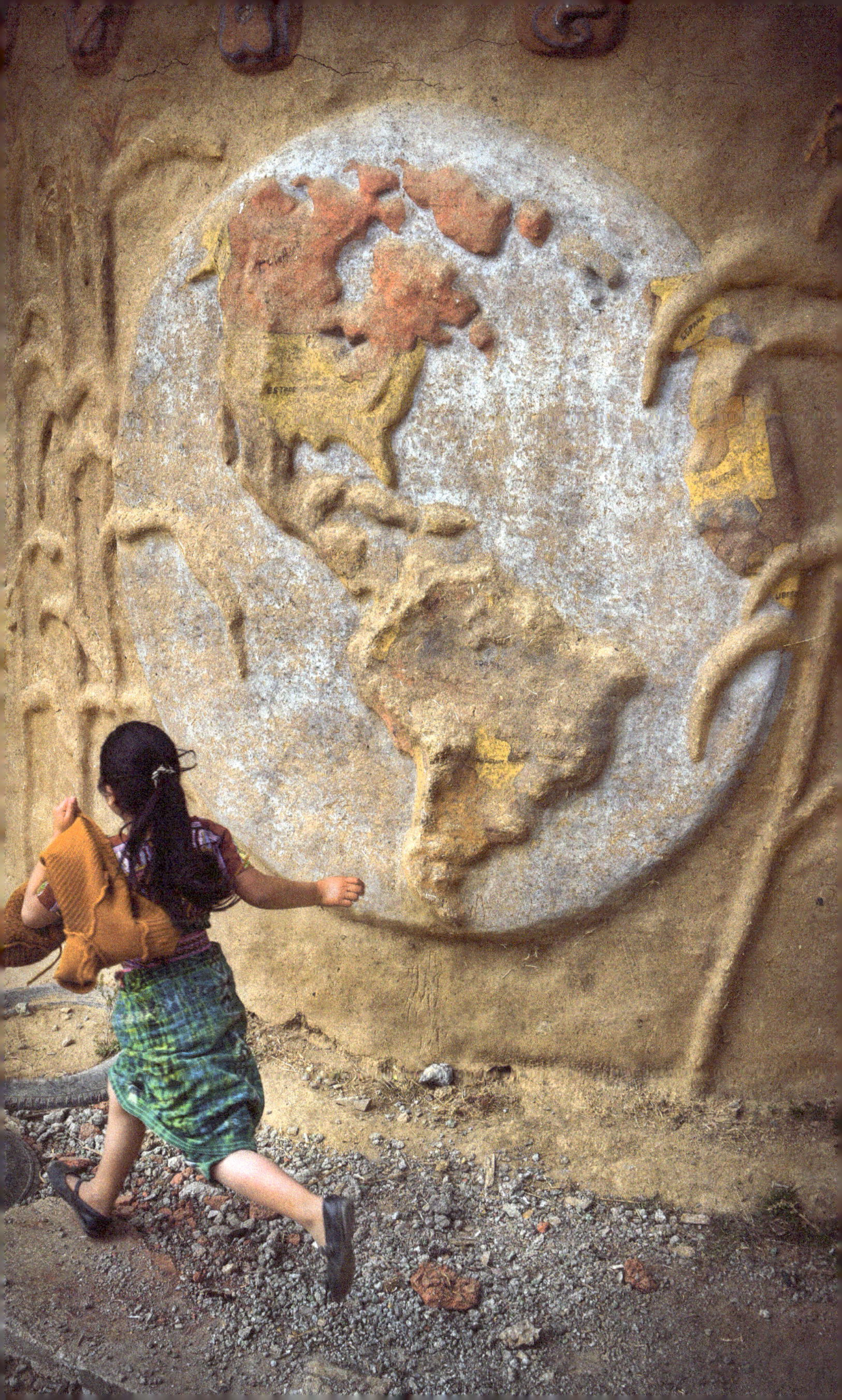

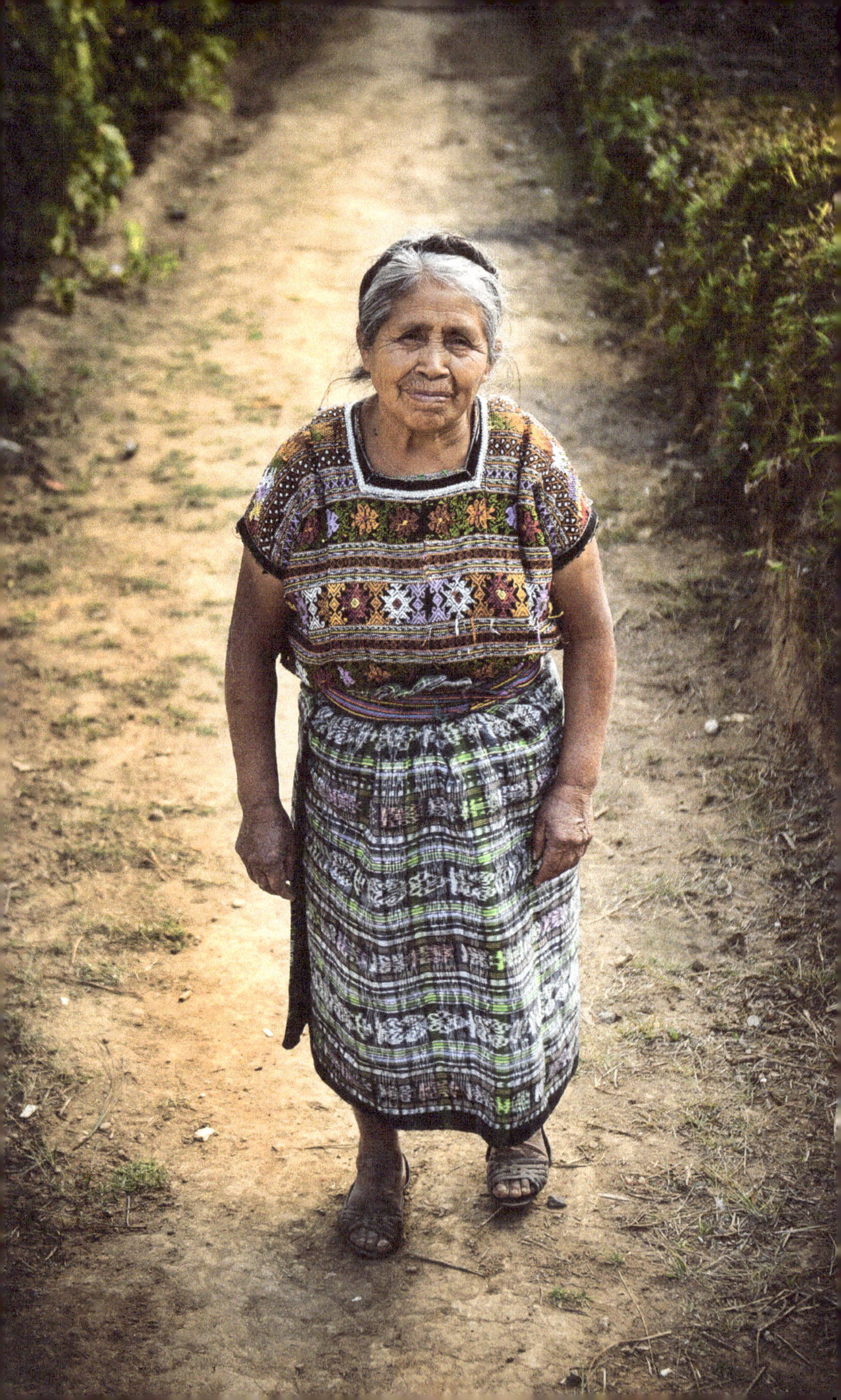

PHOTO TIP: THE BALANCE OF PHOTOGRAPHY

Since education has become a theme of my travels, I wanted to implement that same theme in this book—in a practical way. Part of my goal is to help aspiring photographers better understand the craft, and to address non-photographers by weaving in broader lessons I've learned from this business.

For those reasons, I want to briefly cover the basics of photography. Yes, as I mentioned earlier, these rules may be obvious to some of you—but even if you're familiar with the concepts, as in any specialty, it's helpful to refresh your memory. Rarely is anyone a perfect master of the basics in any art, science or hobby. Sometimes you'll discover a new take on an old subject.

The fundamentals of photography work in tandem with one another. Together, they create an ecosystem that must be carefully balanced, and a good photographer knows how to balance them swiftly and without hesitation. One change will often require another.

When it comes to the fundamentals of photography, three aspects matter more than anything else: aperture, shutter speed and ISO. These are the three core pillars of any image and will determine what your shot looks like—and how well you can see it.

The aperture is literally the hole in the lens through which light travels into the camera, hitting the digital sensor or film. It acts like the iris of the human eye, widening and tightening, depending on the light conditions. The larger the aperture of the lens—the wider the hole—the more light enters the camera. In photography, an aperture is expressed in "F" numbers, also known as F-stops, which are used to describe how wide or tight the aperture is. These numbers are often what confuse photography newbies: a *smaller* F-stop actually represents a *larger* aperture, such as F/1.4. A larger F-stop, like F/22, represents a smaller aperture.

Aside from allowing the amount of light to pass through the lens, the aperture has an impact on the depth of field. If you want a certain part of your image to be sharp and other parts blurry—or, conversely, if you want everything to be sharp—you're going to be dealing with aperture. An F-stop like that F/22 I just mentioned will bring all of the foreground and background objects into focus together; this is great for landscapes or candid street photos, when you need to cast a wide net. On the other hand, an F-stop such as F/1.4 will isolate the subject in either the foreground or the background, blurring everything else.

That gently fuzzy background is called bokeh—it's fun to play around with if you have something interesting in the background, like fairy lights or a long forest trail. Different lenses offer different types of bokeh, and it's one way to make your photos really stand out. Wide apertures are common for shooting portraits, since you don't want a crisp background distracting from your subject. I like to focus on my subjects' eyes, since they are, as they say, the window to a person's soul.

There's an old photography expression: "F/8 and be there." The phrase dictates the importance of being present, of meeting the moment and being there to document it. It's basically what photojournalism is all about. But note the first half, too: F/8 is a middle-ground aperture that works in most scenarios, especially if you're shooting something unpredictable. The expression is a little gruff, a little old-timey, but there's wisdom in its simplicity.

Next, let's move on to shutter speed. This is like a door at the end of a dark hallway—once the door (or shutter) is opened, light enters and hits the sensor. The shutter speed is the speed at which the shutter opens and closes. It is the total time that the camera's sensor is exposed to light, measured in fractions of a second. For most shots, if you don't want them to be blurry, 1/500 (which is $1/500^{th}$ of a second) is fine. A one-second shutter would be quite long, and that can result in a blurry photo unless you're shooting something totally still with a tripod and want a blurry effect—think of a waterfall or river in an otherwise still landscape.

Another opportunity for long exposures comes at night. Nighttime photography demands a slow shutter speed, when the shutter is open for multiple seconds or even minutes. There isn't enough light to see anything otherwise. That's why you'll find a lot of nighttime shots with streaking stars or cars that transform into laser beams zipping along a highway—it's stylish, sure, but also usually the only option available.

I recommend experimenting with shutter speeds if you're unfamiliar. Slower shutter speeds can be used to show a sense of motion or movement, even in daylight. (You'll have to adjust your aperture and ISO to darken the image, because a longer exposure will let in much more light.) Water is a good one to practice on: you'll get distinctly different results whether you keep your exposure open for one second, 1/200 or 1/2000. Do you want to see every last drop, or would you rather all the liquid flows together in a blurry stream? There's no wrong answer. It's all about your personal preferences.

If you pan your camera at the same speed of a passing car using a slow shutter speed, the car will appear sharp while giving a motion blur to the background. When I'm photographing sports, like surfing, I need a very high shutter speed. Depending on the length of my lens, I would start with a shutter speed of at least 1/2000. Most cameras have shutter speeds as high as 1/8000.

The final pillar of photography for getting a proper exposure is the ISO. ISO is the level of sensitivity in your camera. The lower the ISO, such as 100, the less sensitive it is to light. The higher the ISO, such as 1600, the more sensitive it is to light. With increased sensitivity, the camera can capture images in low light without using a flash.

One thing to be aware of is that with a higher ISO comes more grain or noise in your photos. For the best image quality, use a lower ISO, but when that is not possible because you are trying to get a well-exposed photo without a lot of natural light (like indoors, or in the evening), you'll have to raise your ISO. When I want to keep the amount of noise out of my photos, I always balance my camera on a steady flat surface or put it on a tripod and use a longer exposure, rather than bump up the grain on my camera.

Note that some digital cameras today will shoot what appear to be incredibly clear images in fairly low light. That's because the most sensitive film ISO was 1600. (It's also worth mentioning that traditional film ISO levels were set in doubled amounts: 100, 200, 400, 800, 1600.) Today, that concept has been surpassed by leaps and bounds. Not only can cameras shoot unique ISOs in between those amounts, but they can jack the ISO all the way up to ridiculous amounts like 6400, 12,800 or even 25,600. (A few years ago, Canon introduced a $30,000 camera whose ISO can go up to *four million*, to give you a sense of where technology is taking us.) It's worth noting that the quality of images can remain impressively sharp even at ISO 3200, since the quality of the camera sensors and number of megapixels has increased so much in the last decade, so some of the stigma of high ISOs is fading away. Crazy-high ISO is still fine for Instagram, but if you're printing your work for a client, it's better to keep it safer and sharper with a lower ISO. Besides, if you're shooting in the daytime, you probably won't need to go above 1600 too often anyway.

The ISO, shutter speed and aperture all make up the exposure of an image. How you navigate all three is where the balance lies: it's a careful consideration, depending on your location, the mood you're going for and how much light is available.

To sum it up, photography is the art of balance. You're balancing light and dark; textures and colors; weight and composition. The best artists have a natural knack for understanding this balance. But by studying the science behind the art, you can unlock the secret, and begin seeing the craft in a whole new light.

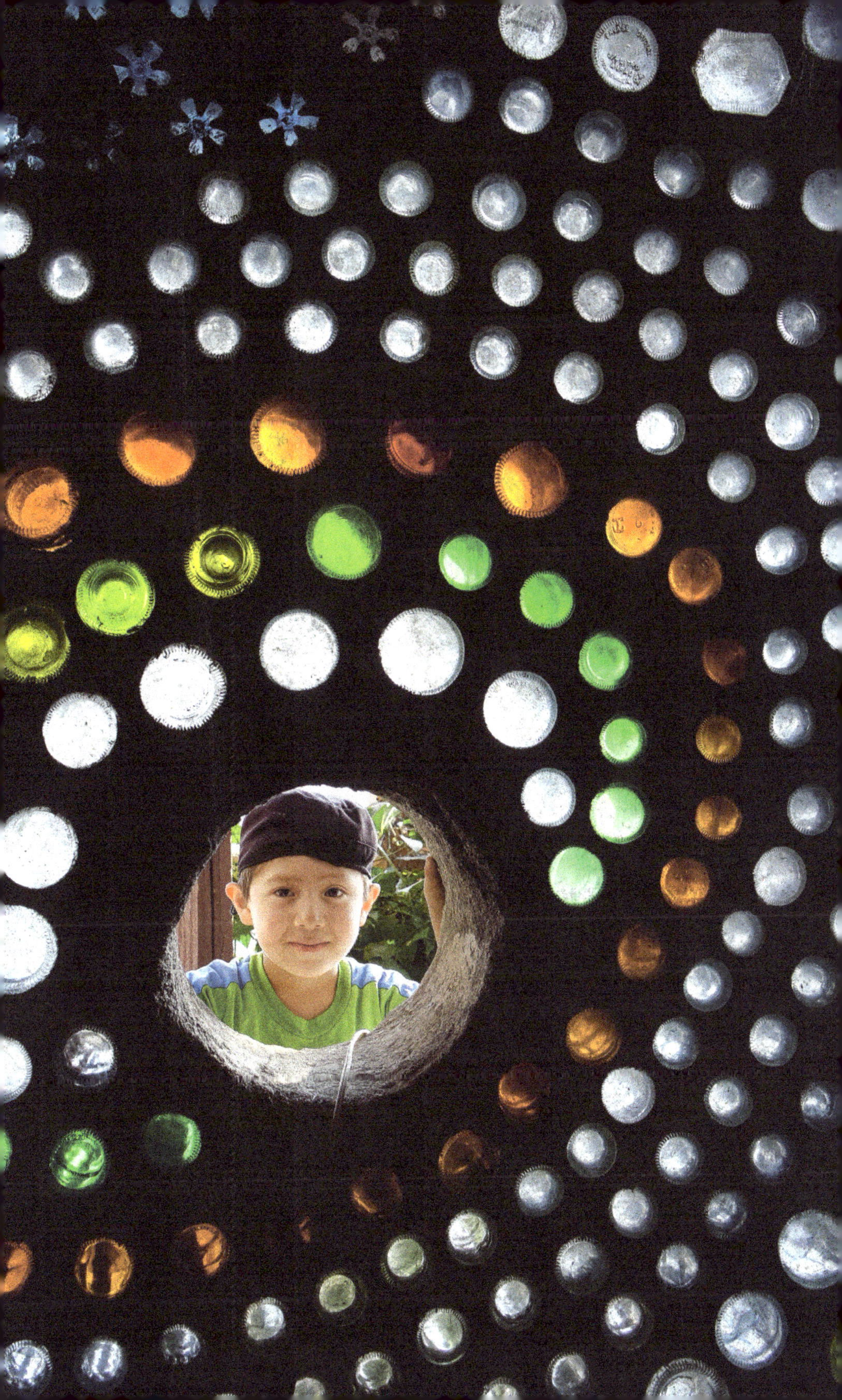

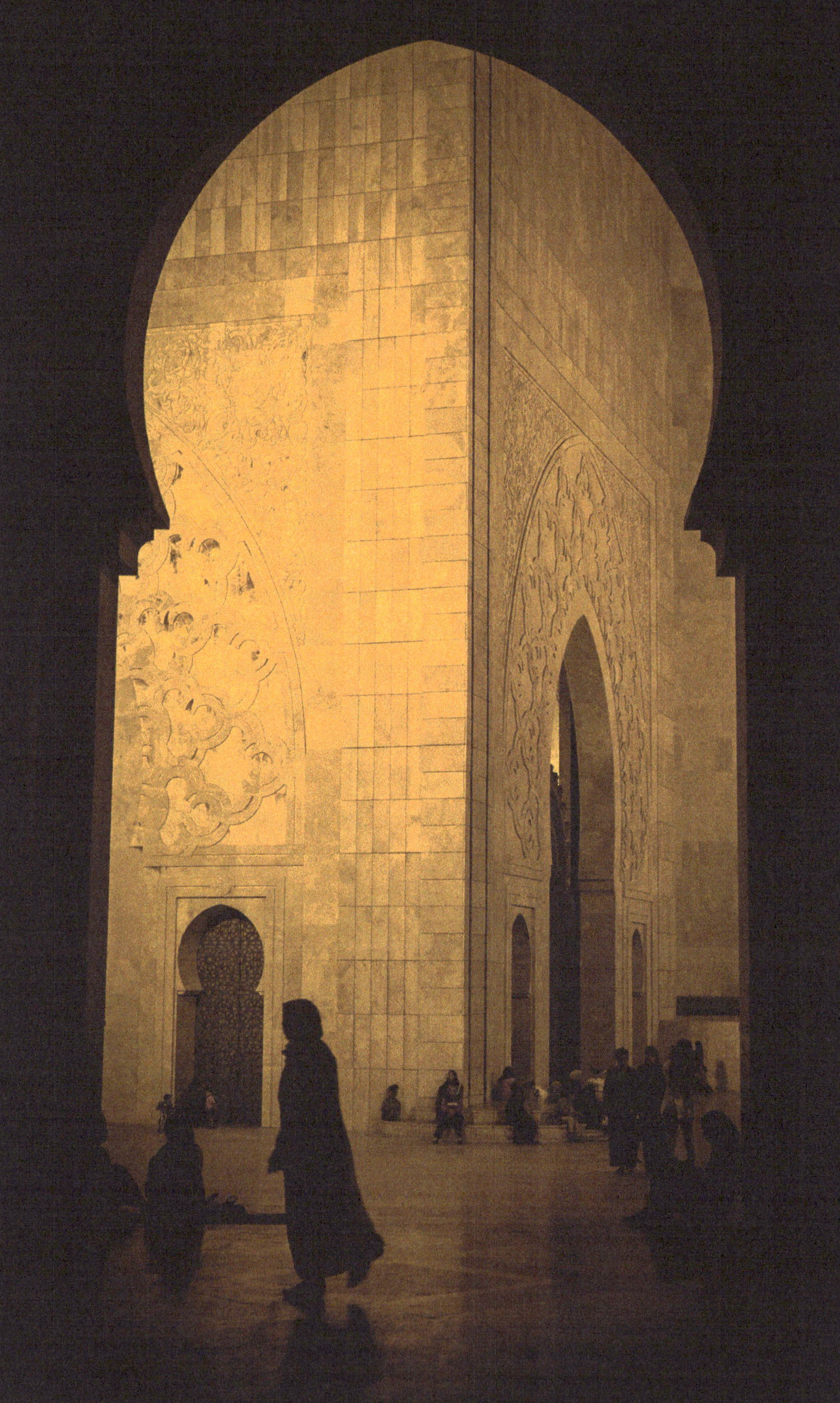

CHAPTER 4

FLOATING THROUGH MOROCCO

"You will become as small as your controlling desire; as great as your dominant aspiration."
– James Allen

Sandy coastlines stretch for hundreds of miles. The waves of the Atlantic Ocean gracefully crash ashore. Ornate mosaic patterns mesmerize the eyes. Rugged mountains boom behind me, forming the interior of the colorful and vibrant Kingdom of Morocco.

Bordering the Sahara Desert to the south and the Mediterranean coast to the north, Morocco is a physically diverse country at the northwestern tip of Africa, pointing directly to Spain. Filled with rich history and stunning Islamic architecture, multilingual residents (both French and Arabic are taught here) and hearty Arab food, the country is as hypnotic as it is impressive. I could sit in a café in the "Pink City" of Marrakesh for hours, sipping well sugared mint tea and watching the world unfold before me, crowds mingling around the mystical medina and lush gardens.

The grand spectacle of the Jemaa el-Fna, a popular central marketplace in Marrakesh, draws locals and tourists in with mesmerizing aromas, spirited banter and intense haggling. The swooping Saharan dunes shift imperceptibly every day, whisked up with the wind. The high peaks of the Atlas Mountains, crossing into Algeria and Tunisia in the north, tell stories older than human history.

Morocco's inhabitants are wonderfully diverse. In the mountain ranges, the Amazigh tribes (commonly called Berbers, though they don't like that term—it was given to them by Europeans and literally means "barbarian") live in classic adobe homes, relying on camels for transport and crafting world-class pieces of pottery and jewelry. Carpet-weaving and henna art are also proud traditions here. When you meet these locals, with their traditions so firmly intact and turbans wrapped tightly to protect them from the sun, you understand firsthand what makes Arab hospitality so world-class: they will offer you tea, perhaps a snack, a seat and whatever conversation they can manage.

I was privileged to spend a couple of days with a local family I connected with on Airbnb. I was just looking for a clean bed and hot shower, but I stumbled upon much more. My host family was beyond welcoming; even despite our language barrier, we managed to converse for hours about family, the king of Morocco, tea, weddings, surfing, Barack Obama, religion, freedom and life in general. They struck me as genuinely curious, insightful people.

I wasn't their only guest. The local mosque happened to be next door and was undergoing renovations during my stay. Local men used the first floor of this house, where I was staying, as a temporary place of prayer, laying down rugs and bowing toward Mecca multiple times each day. That, of course, was not advertised among the amenities on Airbnb.

I found observing their rituals enlightening, because many Americans stigmatize Muslim people, especially after 9/11. That day was profoundly traumatic for myself and millions of other Americans, but spending time in Morocco among a community filled with nothing but peace and well-wishes resonated deeply with me. Morocco is an ocean away on another continent. Yet deep down, we are all human beings; we all want to learn, live our lives in peace, raise our children and watch them grow. As travelers, we can only take out of an experience what we put into it, and it's incumbent on us to put our whole selves in, to learn as much as we can.

Beyond the borders of this town, snow falls in the highest reaches of the Atlas Mountains. The serenity of this landscape is articulated by the year-round rivers that flow from the mountains toward the cities and villages below, transforming valleys into fertile land for agriculture and, today, major urban and rural centers.

History is palpable in Morocco, and it's a history worth

remembering. These people fought for independence against the French in the 1950s and won, becoming one of the earliest decolonized nations of the 20th century. This appreciation for independence dates back even further. I only learned this after my visit, but in December 1777, Morocco's sultan actually became the first head of state in the world to acknowledge the new United States of America as a legal country. The two nations formalized relations a decade later. We're old friends.

My visit to Morocco was crowned by a short stay in the beautiful city of Casablanca. With more than three million inhabitants, it is by far the largest city in the country, graced by rich Arabic culture, a lofty economic status (it's the chief port on the beautiful Atlantic Ocean) and the fame of the classic movie that bears its name. Casablanca is like New York or Toronto: it's not the national capital, but it's the financial, cultural and economic center. In this case, major banks and industries are headquartered in Casablanca, while massive malls, football arenas and theaters keep people entertained.

But it would be a mistake to visit Morocco and only see the big cities of Casablanca, Rabat and Marrakesh. Farther south, a small fishing village called Taghazout, about 25 miles north of the city of Agadir, held some of the most pristine beaches I'd seen in my life. The local economy relies on fishing, tourism and the production of argan oil, a native oil that's used for dipping and drizzling on flatbreads and couscous. But the beaches are what drew me there: on my last day a big swell attracted surfers to the warm salty waters, and the desert sun broke through the clouds, silhouetting these athletes against an endless ocean.

It's not surprising that so many famous writers have become enchanted with Morocco over the years. The country is silky-smooth and rough, tranquil yet wild. Casablanca hosts a famous book fair every February, no doubt bolstered by the sheer number of Western literary titans who've flourished here. Tennessee Williams wrote *Cat on a Hot Tin Roof* in Morocco; the classic Beat Generation novelist William S. Burroughs penned *Naked Lunch* in a hotel in Tangier. George Orwell, Jack Kerouac, Mark Twain and, most famously, Paul Bowles have all traveled to Morocco in search of inspiration—and all have found it.

I'm no George Orwell, but Morocco definitely inspired me just as well. It actually marked the beginning of my travel blog, *Art, Style, Flow*, which began as short blog posts to fill in the gaps between photos. Eventually, that blog evolved into a vehicle for longer stories; then I turned it into a magazine. Now, those words inspired the very book you're reading.

And it all started in Morocco. There's something magical about this place—but to understand, you have to see it for yourself.

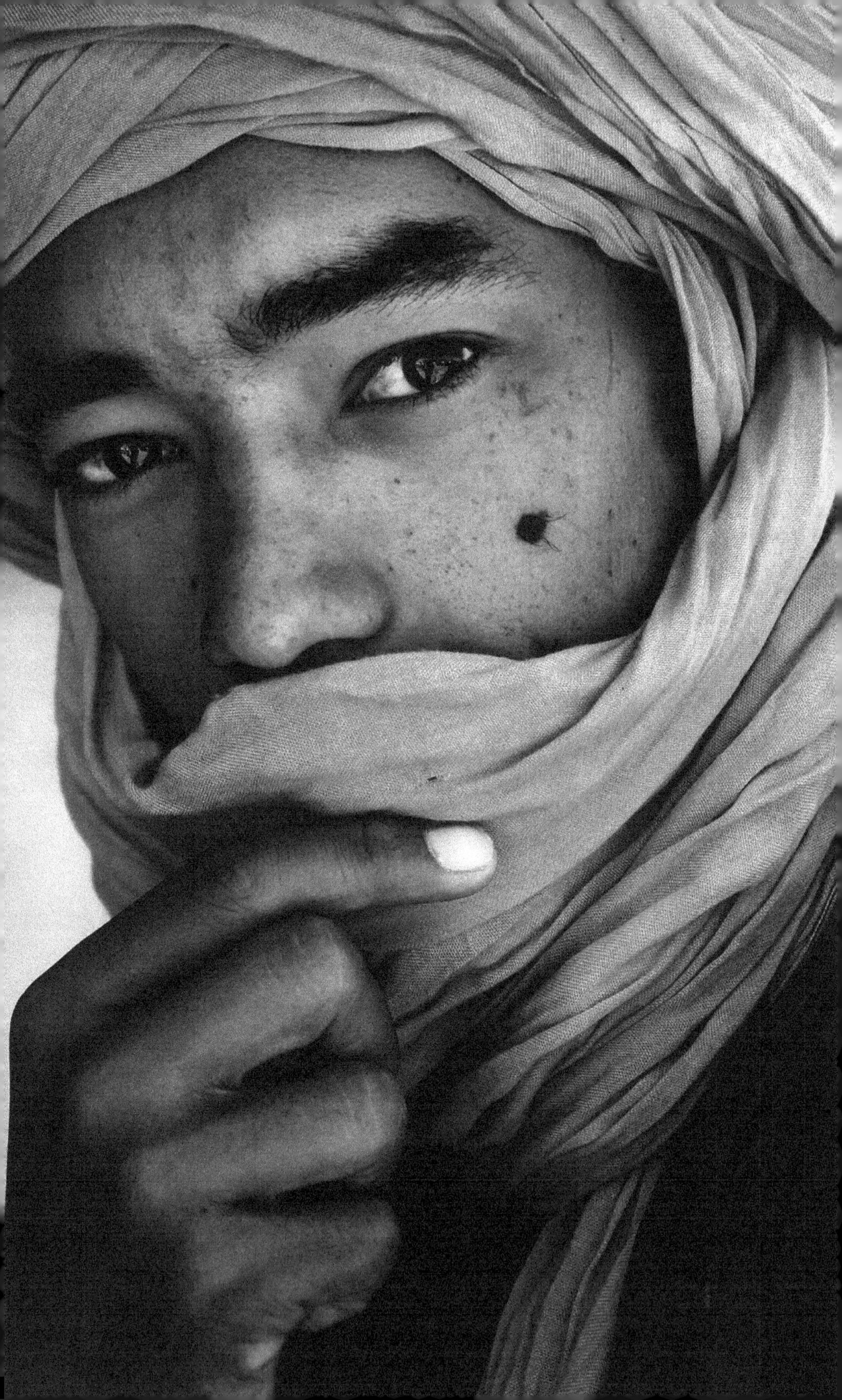

TRAVEL TIP: DEALING WITH JET LAG

After traveling to places like Morocco, Guatemala and beyond, I've developed a few techniques for dealing with jet lag and making the most of your travels.

Jet lag is when your circadian rhythm—your internal clock—doesn't have time to adjust to a new time zone. If you've just arrived in India at night, your body will still think it's that same morning back in North America. It can take days to fully adapt and, in the meantime, your vacation will be interrupted by lengthy daytime naps and staring at your hotel room ceiling at 4 a.m.

So if you're hoping to mitigate your jet lag frustrations, either en route to your destination or on your way back home, here are a few tips that have personally helped me during my travels.

1. **Adjust your schedule before departing.** Make a note of which direction you're heading. If you're traveling from east to west, try to delay your body clock so you get up and go to sleep later. If you're heading eastward, I've found this can be more difficult. Regardless, even changing your body clock by an hour or two will help the eventual transition.

2. **Do not drink a lot of caffeine, alcohol or other stimulants.** You might think downing coffee will help keep you awake. If it affects you at all, it will be temporary; besides, caffeine doesn't completely escape your system for up to 10 hours, so you might be doing yourself more harm than good.
3. **Regulate your exposure to light.** Blackout curtains and nightlights can help with this. When traveling westward, avoid morning light if possible, and instead try to get extra afternoon light. Do the opposite if you're heading east.
4. **Don't bother trying to adjust if you're only gone for a short time.** It's not worth it, especially if you're not flying more than three time zones. You're probably better off remaining on your home time.
5. **Pick a flight that arrives early in the day.** It's obviously easier to sleep on a red-eye flight and arrive in the morning, regardless of which direction you're heading. Your sleep might not be great—maybe just a few hours, even though you're now 12 hours ahead—but you can slog through that first day and reset at night.
6. **Give yourself an extra day.** This is the most important rule for me: for logistic reasons, as well as your circadian rhythm, never book tight flights if you have assignments or commitments to make. Give yourself *at least* one full day to relax, recuperate and gather your thoughts. This is both

for going away and coming back. I hate returning home on a Sunday and heading to work on Monday—I'm often dazed and confused anyway, and not much good to anyone.

As a quick follow-up to that last tip, how you use that downtime is up to you. I personally like to focus on relaxation and regrouping my thoughts. That, and planning my next adventure. Where are you heading next?

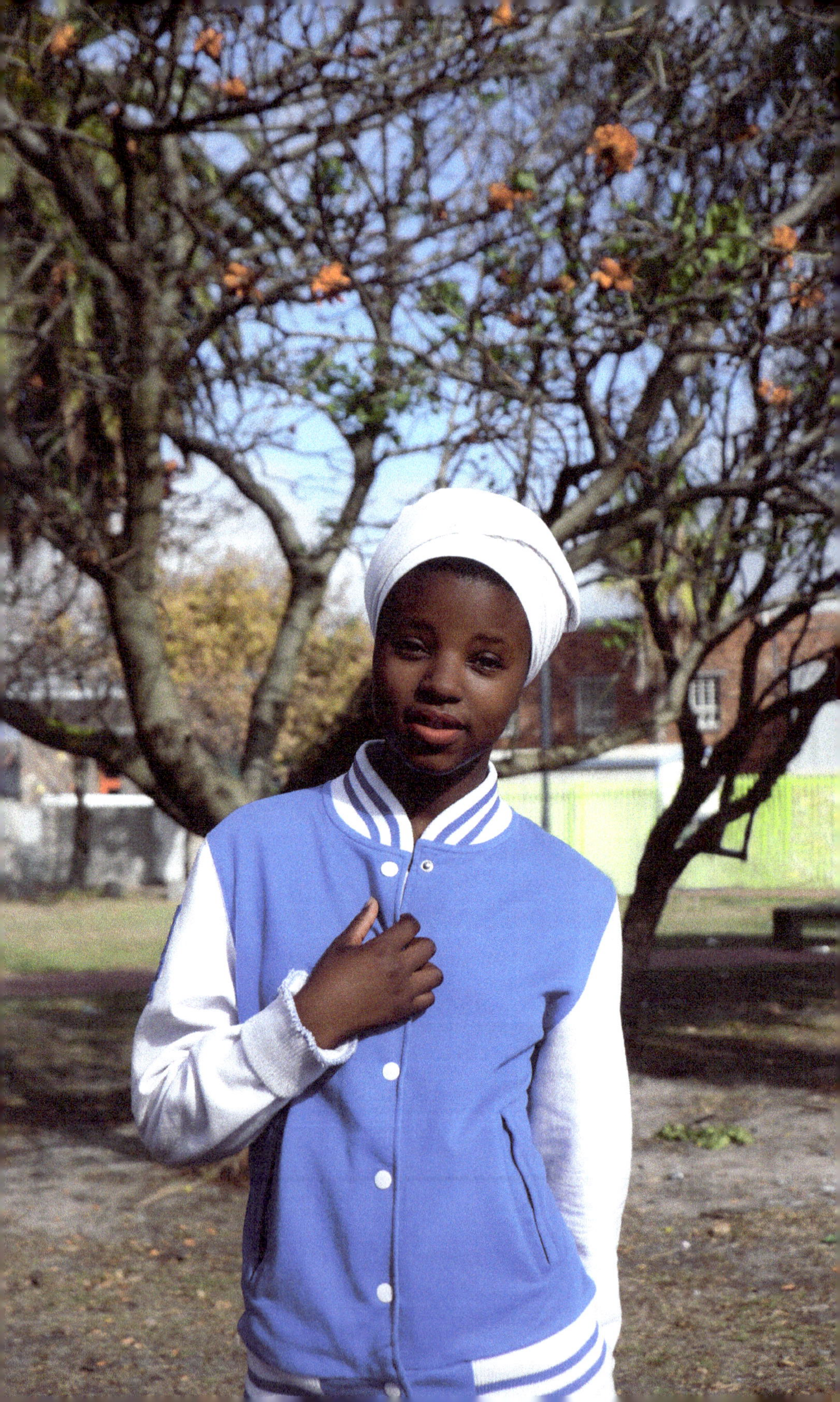

CHAPTER 5

ALL SMILES IN BOTSWANA

"Human dignity, like justice and freedom, is the common heritage of all men. It is indivisible."
– Sir Seretse Khama

In the 1960s, Botswana was a new nation full of postcolonial promise. Its first president was a man named Seretse Khama, who proudly defied his racist apartheid neighbors by marrying a white British woman and developing his small, landlocked country without authoritarianism or discrimination. The Botswanans loved Khama, and his name belongs up in the history books with Nelson Mandela and Mahatma Gandhi.

Khama oversaw the early transition of Botswana from an impoverished, rural nation into one of the strongest democracies in Africa. His government created a new city, Gaborone, near the border with South Africa, to house the nation's capital. In 1964, when Gaborone swung open its doors to the world, it had just under 4,000 residents. Today, it has more than 200,000—one tenth of the total population of Botswana. It's the country's cultural, commercial and administrative capital, with many wildlife refuges and nature reserves.

Gaborone was also my second destination with Photographers Without Borders. About a year after my Guatemala trip, I found an assignment in the southern African nation with a youth-focused NGO that would take me to the capital for two weeks.

I flew from Florida to New York, then to South Africa and up to Botswana. The whole journey took nearly 30 hours, and I spent every minute bursting with anticipation. As I stepped off the small commuter plane in sub-Saharan Africa, I was greeted by two things: an intensely dry heat and a welcome party of two people from the NGO.

The NGO was called Young 1ove (yes, that's how it's spelled), and the two staffers who picked me up were named Olerato and Dot. Their smiles were so infectious that, despite my jet lag, all I wanted in that moment was to grab lunch with them. I dined on a delicious fresh shrimp salad while we got to know each other, soaking in our mutual excitement. We spent the rest of the day discussing politics, laughing at things we had in common (and things we didn't), generating ideas for my time in Botswana and going over the neighborhoods of Gaborone. We even squeezed in an event at the National Stadium, where I was granted VIP access to stand alongside the local press and snap photos of some of the country's top music artists.

When I could no longer hold my eyes open, we said a brief goodbye. Really, it was more of a “see you soon,” because in just a few short hours I’d be back in their company at the Young 1ove head office.

YOUNG 1OVE WAS FOUNDED with an ethical goal grounded in data. They send speakers to schools across the country to give presentations on the realities behind HIV infection, sexual activity and teenage pregnancy. Specifically, they talk about the danger of young girls dating older men, who are more likely to be HIV-positive.

Having lived for many years in New York City, I’ve seen firsthand what HIV and AIDS can do to people. We’re lucky to live in a country where treatments are readily available, and people with the virus can still live rich, fulfilling lives. But in Botswana, those treatments aren’t as readily accessible, and the costs are much higher.

Botswana is one of the hardest-hit countries when it comes to HIV and AIDS. In the last decade alone, the number of Botswanans with AIDS shot up from 290,000 in 2005 to 320,000 in 2013, despite numerous efforts by the government and NGOs like Young 1ove. It’s a constant uphill battle, which makes every on-the-ground effort that much more meaningful.

My first full day at the office was difficult, mostly because I needed to quickly adjust to the six-hour time difference. But the thrill of getting to work and meeting everyone was more than enough to get me moving on that brisk morning. Inside the office, I realized that special smile I'd first noticed on Olerato and Dot—it wasn't just them. Everyone smiled that way, full of genuine happiness and sincerity. Maybe it's a Botswanan thing, or maybe it's a Young 1ove thing. Either way, it was something special, and it made me feel completely welcome and inspired.

The day started with my official welcome, "Young 1ove–style," which was held outside. Everyone stood in a big circle to play a concentration game mixed with light exercise, all played to the beat of our snapping fingers, led by Thato, who goes by Miss Tee. I later learned that Miss Tee would play a central role in my story—but more on that in a minute.

Playing this game first thing in the morning served many purposes. Mostly, it was to get our bodies and minds moving, but it also gave us an icebreaker moment to bond with each other, laugh and—most of all—smile.

I spent the first few days getting to know all the staff members. I sat on the comfy office couch with each one of them, one at a time, as if we were on a late-night talk show. We chatted about their jobs, their hometowns, the United States and so much more. Their diverse staff hailed from not just around Botswana, but also

England, Canada and the U.S. Although all of them were uniquely charming, they somehow shared a special quality that seemed to perfectly place them in Botswana at Young 1ove. I was surprised that, after only a few days, I felt I belonged there, too.

The mission of Young 1ove is to connect youth with life-saving information about HIV and AIDS. All this work starts in the office, where they comprehensively analyze every single aspect of their organization, from talking points to end goals, and discuss what they want the outcome of each project and discussion to look like. This staff, led by co-founders Noam Angrist and Moitshepi Matsheng, were the most talented, creative and hardworking group I'd ever met. So many moving parts, so many levels, so many narratives.

Now it was my turn: I needed to get to work on my angle for telling their story.

On my first project for PWB in Guatemala, I was working with a school being constructed out of recyclable items like old tires and colorful glass bottles, and there were 118 adorable kids running around every day. I had no trouble finding intriguing characters and funky details to photograph. In Botswana, on the other hand, I spent most of my time in an office. At first, this made it challenging for me to find creative images to shoot, but in the end, I realized that just being present for their meetings, hearing about the statistics of the research they were compiling, being involved in the daily team-bonding sessions and even spending time with some of the staff outside of the office was a fascinating behind-the-scenes look at how profoundly good work is done. Ultimately, these meetings became a core tenet of my story.

On my first Sunday in Gaborone, this vision became much clearer as I spent the morning with Miss Tee at her church outside of the city. Then I saw them again: those charming smiles! There they were on children's freshly washed faces, throughout the congregation, in the choir and on the minister—but especially within the spirit of my host for the day, Miss Tee.

At that time, I still didn't fully understand Miss Tee's role at Young 1ove, but what I did find out that morning was that she was a genuine, caring and respected person in her community. I would later learn just how she brought those traits to her work and the impact on people's lives that she was capable of.

Before I knew it, my second week had begun, and we were finally scheduled to go into "the field." This was my opportunity to see how the Young 1over staffers culminate all their detailed work into real life.

I gathered all my camera equipment and joined six staff members for a three-hour drive outside the city in a combi, which is basically a minibus that's commonly used for public transit in Botswana. Driving through small villages and rural landscapes along the way opened my eyes to the wonders of this beautiful country beyond its capital city. I watched locals sell their goods on the side of the street, men walk their livestock down the dusty road and children laugh as they traipsed home from school. Most of my travel-mates were pretty quiet on the drive, but I hadn't noticed, because I rode in the front seat beside the driver and was enraptured by this new foreign film playing before my eyes. Only later did I learn that the staffers were all spending their time studying their presentation materials or quietly meditating to prepare themselves for the afternoon.

As soon as we arrived at the concrete school building, we pulled up along a rust-colored dirt road to meet the headmaster, who greeted us personally and walked us to the classrooms. Outside Gaborone, virtually everything is rural; this school, like many others, was principally concrete and sand. What little greenery there was looked thirsty. Some windows were cracked and broken, while old, empty cork boards hung on the gently crumbling walls. None of this, of course, stopped teachers from doing their best: a simple piece of chalk and ancient chalkboard seemed to be all they needed, and the staff from Young 1ove didn't bring too much more.

On my visit, Miss Tee was to lead one class, while Lorato—for the first time ever—would be leading another down the hall at the same time. Sarah, Gaby and Shayla, who work in Young 1ove's curriculum department, would quietly evaluate some of the new teaching techniques being incorporated that day and compare the seasoned work of Miss Tee to that of newly promoted Lorato. Olerato guided me toward what she felt would be the most visually interesting parts of the presentation and made sure I was in the right place during the simultaneous sessions.

Because their talks focus on young people, and especially women, the in-class instructors are usually young as well, making them more relatable to students. Each session begins with the kids clearing out the middle of the classroom and moving their heavy, well-used desks and chairs to the sides of the room. The instructor gathers everyone in a circle and leads them through a series of exercises and memory games to get them relaxed and engaged. It reminded me of my welcome on that first day, and I realized that might not be a coincidence.

I loved watching Miss Tee and Lorato present in front of so many beaming, exuberant children. At first, I thought their speeches were ad-libbed, but later realized all their words and moves were carefully chosen and choreographed to optimize the process in a short amount of time.

Once the kids were comfortable, the instructors gave out a little information about why they were there and the importance of the subject matter.

They tie together the three themes of HIV/AIDS, teen pregnancy and dating older men. One of their goals is to inform students that older men have higher rates of HIV infection than younger people, and that dating an age-appropriate person is much safer than dating someone significantly older. The phenomenon of older guys dating teenagers or 20-somethings is sometimes called being a "sugar daddy," and exists in North America as well, especially among college students looking for extra cash to fund their tuition and nights out. In sub-Saharan Africa, sugar daddies are mainly about status and luxury. A survey of 600 girls in Gaborone, published in 2006, found that 79 percent of the respondents who were in relationships with older men frankly said they did it because the men are "able to provide gifts and money." Older men are seen as safer partners, too, because of their emotional maturity, financial stability and life experience.

The problem is that older men have much higher rates of HIV/AIDS than younger men, simply (and logically) because they have had more sexual partners. To illustrate this, the Young 1ove presenters created an exercise they conduct in each session. They separate the class into four groups and give them a disassembled graph of HIV rates and ages. Then, they ask the kids to organize the graph, based on what statistics they think are correct matches.

When the groups finish their graphs, one or two students from each group are asked to stand at the front of the classroom and explain their group's logic. Most (if not all) think that 15- to 20-year-olds are the least safe group when it comes to HIV, and those over 40 are less likely to be infected. After each group makes their presentation, the instructor reveals the actual statistical chart: the truth is the complete opposite of what these kids originally thought. The kids are shocked, and Young 1ove's staffers can rest easy knowing their message has been received loud and clear.

It was eye-opening to see the students go from being tired after a long day at school to standing up and dancing with excitement, then be brought back down with a healthy dose of life-saving information. The entire process was carefully orchestrated, and you could see how these students were learning something that could actually change their lives.

The day wrapped up with another game and a reminder of the core message. By the end, all the kids looked at the instructors with pride and gratitude as they filled out questionnaires about what they had learned. Lorato did an amazing job on her first day, but for me, watching Miss Tee in her element was more fascinating. I was reminded of being with her in church, where she was a community staple, and tried to capture some of her warmth with my camera.

I was only able to accompany the crew out in the field one more time during my visit, and it was a different kind of outing. After a few more days back at the Young 1ove headquarters, we headed out of town for a two-day general meeting in a verdant private area. We spent most of the time in stucco buildings topped with grass roofs, like modern huts, where the group took a macro view of their organization. They broke down what was working and what wasn't and came up with creative solutions for what success could look like. In our spare time, we got the chance to spend quality time together, escaping the concrete conference rooms and spreadsheets to enjoy long walks through nature. I marveled at the beautiful golden beams of afternoon sunlight, which granted me some of the best opportunities for beautiful outdoor portraits. The staff, it seemed, were happy to be out of the classroom, out of the office, out of the conference room—finally able to enjoy their beautiful country.

I TOOK ADVANTAGE OF my time in Southern Africa outside of Botswana, too. I didn't intend to visit Cape Town, but a last-minute decision brought me to South Africa's legislative capital. Now I tell everyone to put the city on their bucket list.

I rented a flat near the base of Table Mountain, with a picturesque view of the city that hooked me as soon as I arrived. I spent a day hiking around the narrow, rocky cliffs of Cape Point, the extreme southwestern tip of the African continent, where the Indian and Atlantic oceans meet. It's a little daunting to trek along rocks that hang precariously over churning water below.

A half-hour drive north of the famous Cape of Good Hope Old Lighthouse is Boulders Beach, home to an adorable colony of penguins. I'd never seen a penguin in person before and was surprised to learn they all had different personalities. It was like watching a group of people: some were fighting, some were grooming each other, others kept to themselves. Their spirit was calming and wonderful.

The wildest wildlife I saw, however, came during my four-day stint at a South African safari on designated conservation land, where my finger trembled on my camera's shutter as I snapped photos of the "Big Five" African animals (elephants, rhinoceroses, leopards, cape buffalo and lions), not to mention flocks of zebras and southern yellow-billed hornbills. I even spotted a cheetah lolling about in a tree—there are only around 7,000 of these endangered animals alive today, so when you're lucky enough to spot one, it's hard to take your eyes off of its majestic coat and sleek movements.

While all these experiences were unforgettable, the most affecting moments of my South African excursion dealt with the inevitable, tragic history of racism and apartheid. I mentioned Seretse Khama at the beginning of this chapter—relatively few people know his name, but many more know the name of Nelson Mandela.

Looking at the history of Botswana and South Africa side-by-side is jarring. While Botswana enjoyed Khama's principled leadership during pivotal postcolonial years, Mandela's tenure as president wouldn't come until decades later, in the mid-1990s. Before that, he was imprisoned at Robben Island, a quick ferry ride from mainland Africa. I visited the jail during my trip and was shocked to see firsthand how wretched his sentence was. He spent 18 years in a small, damp concrete cell, forbidden from hearing much news from the outside world and often thrown in solitary confinement. He worked hard labor, breaking rocks into gravel for so long that his eyesight was permanently damaged afterwards. But Mandela is also a symbol of resilience: he used his time to write, study law and hone his political beliefs. Like Gandhi in India, Mandela proved that violence isn't always necessary. Peaceful protest and education can make the world a better place.

South Africans still have a way to go. Even today, white citizens enjoy significant privileges over the Black population. You can see it in Langa, a poor area of town visited by few tourists—the apartheid government segregated Black people here, and it served as a pivotal area for anti-racist protests and marches. To the west, the District Six Museum is a memorial to the neighborhood of the same name that was razed in the 1970s and '80s, when the apartheid regime declared the neighborhood an irreparable vice den of gambling, prostitution and alcoholism.

But there is good news at the end of all this. It strikes me that Africa's worst days are behind it—I found this to be true in Botswana and South Africa, where an attitude of forward-looking optimism drives locals and community leaders toward great success.

The evidence is in the details. Personally, my most precious memory from Southern Africa came on my last day in Botswana, when I left the Young 1ove office. Upon my departure, the staff presented me with the most special gift: an African basket filled with handwritten notes from each staff member. Tears filled my eyes as I eagerly read each note; they were full of cute sayings, well wishes, special memories and kind words about me and my visit.

I felt a little like a thief to have taken so many great things away from Botswana, and I can only hope that the people I met remember me as fondly as I remember them.

My time in Botswana ended in much the same way it had begun two weeks prior: standing in group circles, laughing to the beat of snapping fingers and, without a doubt, lots of memorable smiles.

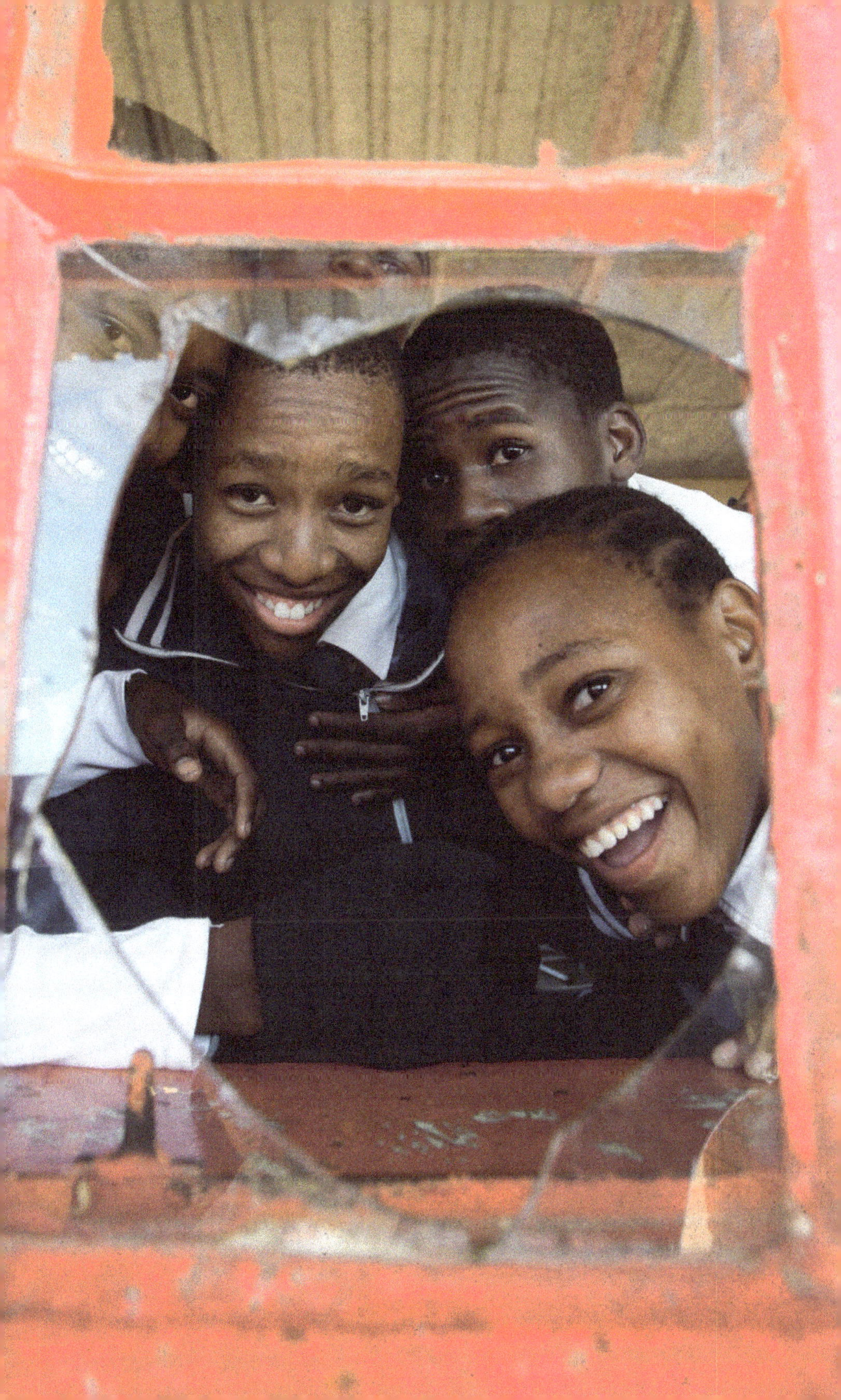

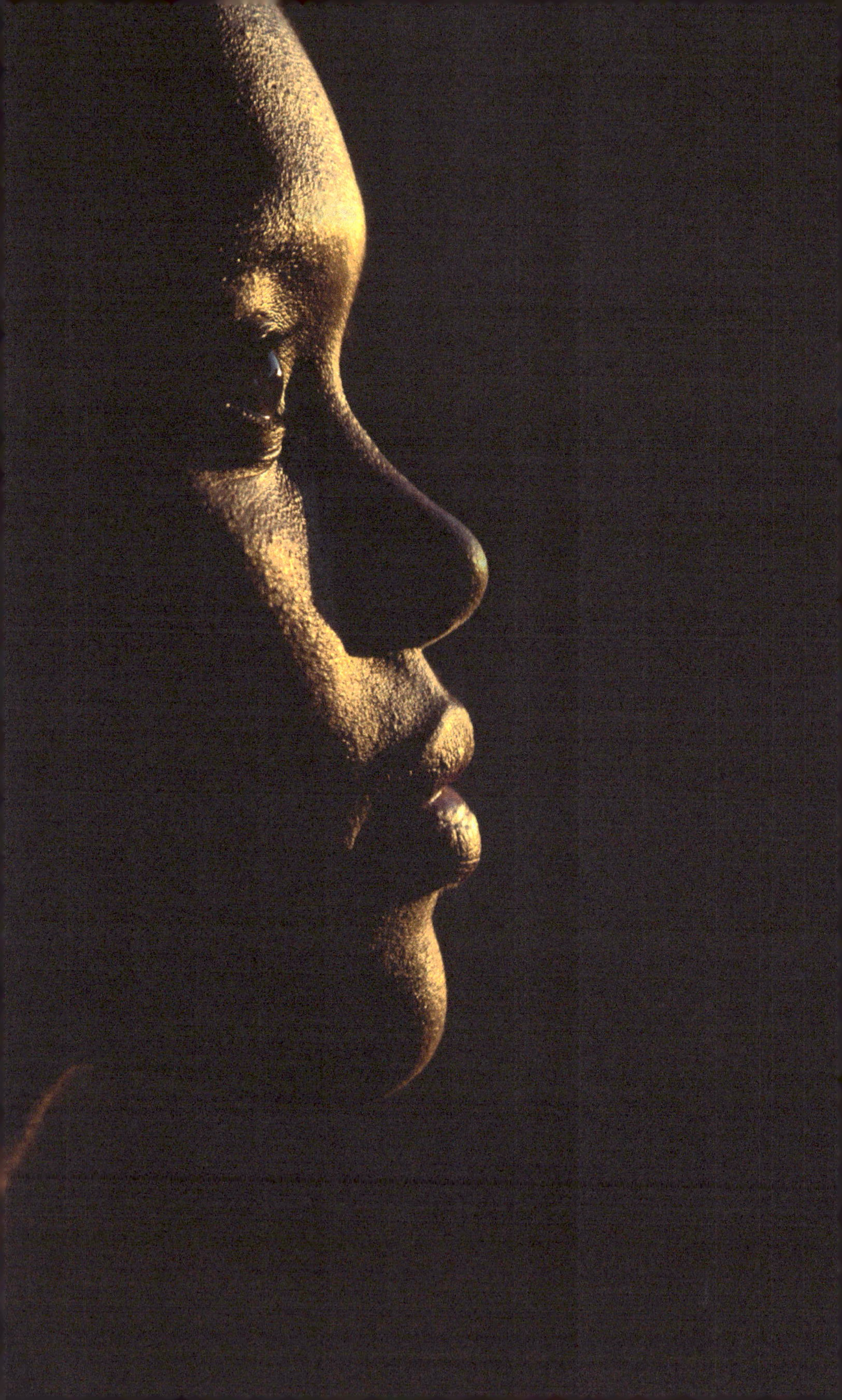

PHOTO TIP: COMPOSITION

It's inevitable. Sometimes, you see something absolutely beautiful—a lion in the sunset, an African jungle flower, a group of children smiling together—and you raise your camera, look at it through your viewfinder, and… it just won't look good.

There's a reason behind the popular expression, "Photos just don't do it justice." The "it" in that sentence is usually something breathtaking and miraculous, whether a natural wonder or manmade monument.

While the balance of ISO, aperture and shutter speed will greatly affect your images, composition matters as much as anything else. In some ways, this is also the easiest trick for anyone to pick up. You don't need a fancy DSLR camera to understand framing. You just need a good eye.

I personally skew toward environmental portraits—portraits of people in their natural environment. I find this gives my images an honesty and authenticity that's hard to beat in a studio. It also makes composition a little easier, since I know that every element in the frame is relevant to my subject's life.

Even with a smartphone, you can create beautiful

compositions. It's all about angles, knowing what to include versus what to exclude. With a strong sense of composition, you can make anything look great, even if all you have to work with is a small concrete room full of students.

One general rule—and this is fundamental to all art, not just photography—is the rule of thirds. This is a compelling compositional method for making photos more dynamic. The rule asserts that artworks look better when composed along imaginary lines that divide the image into thirds, either vertically and/or horizontally. Imagine you're staring at the beach during a purplish sunset: you might divide the photo into thirds, so the sand, the water and the sky each take up around a third of the frame. The colors and composition would look nice, simply and evenly divided.

I almost always incorporate this technique into my work. It's antithetical to the rule of thirds to place subjects in the middle of the frame—sometimes symmetry is good, but you need a balance around them. More often I'll place subjects off to the side, so they take up perhaps one-third or two-thirds of the frame, leaving the rest as negative space.

When composing a shot, you'll also have to consider your point of view. Traditionally, this refers to where the camera is positioned; in my opinion, a photographer's point of view could be described as the life experiences they bring to an assignment. Without even realizing it, a photographer injects their opinions, skills and beliefs into their work.

On a practical level, having a unique point of view means exploring all angles when shooting a subject. That might mean standing on a lower level (like downstairs) and shooting upward, or atop a building for an aerial view, or capturing a shot of my subject through foliage. There are a million ways to photograph the same subject, and it's important to stay flexible and move around when trying to tell a story. Different angles can show different sides of people, and that's a way I can put a personal touch on a photograph.

I realize it might sound silly, but I particularly like the example of shooting subjects from behind some foliage. Having that natural green pop in the foreground, and placing my subject off to the other side of the frame, gives my images a sense of depth. In my travel and environmental portrait photography, I've found this technique gives my images a candid look, as if my subjects aren't posing for the camera. Things look more natural and authentic that way, even though the reality (me crouching behind a shrub) is, ironically, a little contrived. Of course, it's not about the behind-the-scenes mechanics, but about the end result.

I take composition extremely seriously, and I always try to frame up my images in my viewfinder the way I want them to look in the end. This saves me from having to crop them later or spend a lot of time editing them in Photoshop. For me, the fun of photography isn't in the editing—it's in the actual photography.

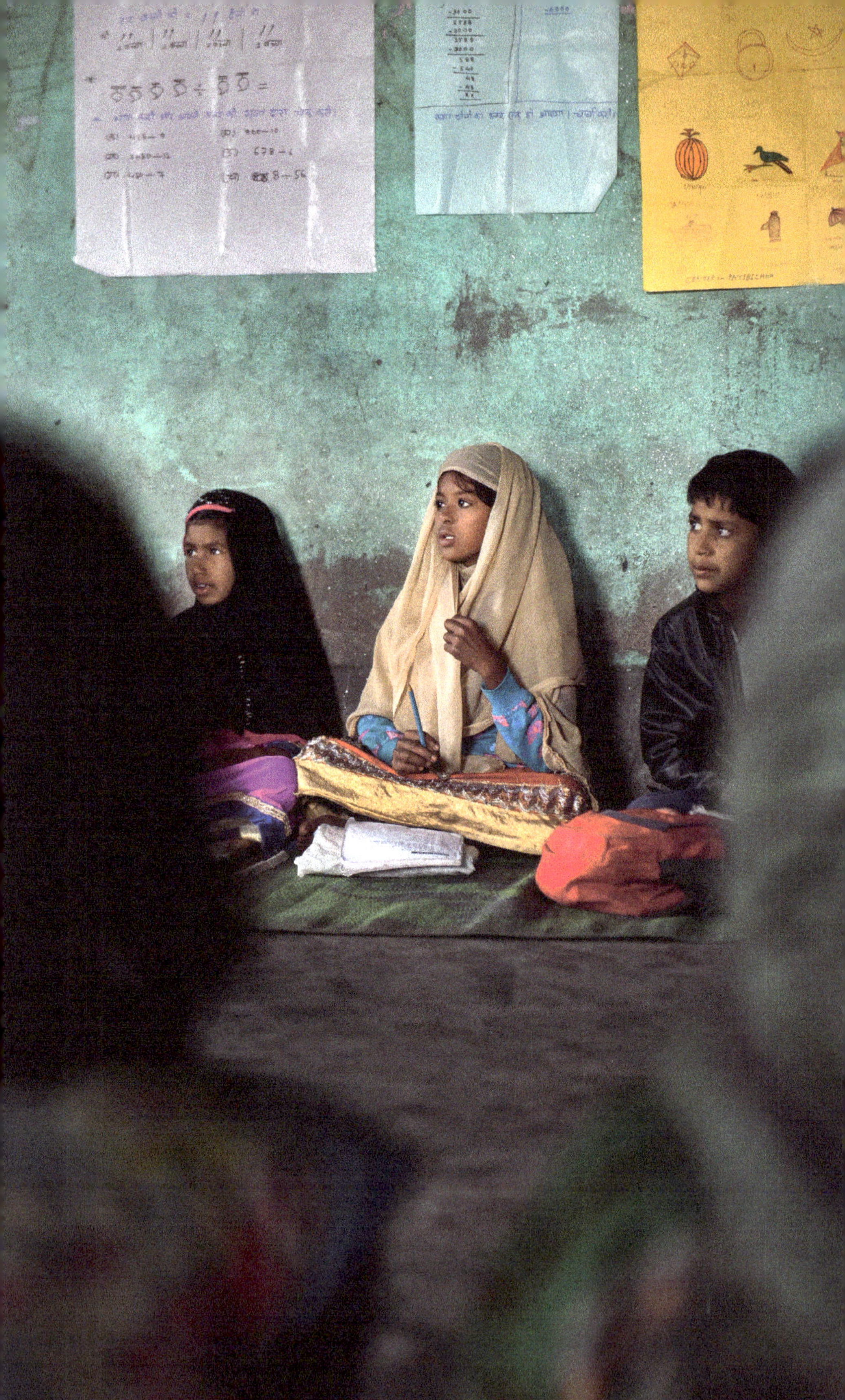

CHAPTER 6

EMERGING FROM THE FOG IN NORTHERN INDIA

"Travel makes one modest. You see what a tiny place you occupy in the world."

– Gustave Flaubert

For the past quarter-century I have been fortunate to travel and tell others' stories, trying to see as much of the world as I can with what I can afford. In those travels, I've visited India more than once—and yet, on my most recent trip to the massive nation, I realized how wrong it is to believe that you've seen a country like India by only going to the big cities like Delhi and Mumbai. To really understand a place, you have to skew off the beaten path and find smaller, less-visited regions, as I did in and around Kishanganj, in the northeastern state of Bihar, on my third assignment for Photographers Without Borders.

Hundreds of years ago, Kishanganj was called Nepalgarh, until India's Mughal Empire invaded and changed the name. It was subsequently absorbed into the British Empire during their colonization in the 1800s. Today, the city of more than 100,000 people, most of whom are Muslim, is one of the most sensitive districts of India, as it sits squarely between the borders of Bangladesh to the east and Nepal to the north. It's less than two hours' drive to either country—this is the slice of Indian territory that bottlenecks between several nations before wrapping back around to Myanmar.

Skirt the Nepalese border heading north, and you'll end up in the lush green hills of Darjeeling in West Bengal. But while Kishanganj isn't as famous as Darjeeling, it still produces tea—in fact, it's the only tea-producing district in the state of Bihar, blessed with abundant fertile land where farmers grow corn, pineapple, okra, cauliflower, cabbage and rice. This gives the whole region a beautiful tranquility that's totally lacking in the big cities.

But this picturesque region is not without its difficulties.

Set at the Himalayan foothills, Kishanganj, like the rest of Bihar, is plagued by severe annual floods. Bihar gets worse and more consistent flooding than anywhere else in India, with more than three-quarters of its population under threat during monsoon season. Rivers overflow their banks; buildings are washed away; cattle drown; crops and livelihoods are destroyed. In the last decade alone, major floods in 2013 and 2017 affected millions of people across dozens of villages, killing hundreds.

Although I had been to India a couple times before, this trip felt different from the start—more special, more rare. Aside from telling stories with my camera, I felt like I had to really concentrate on listening to locals, even though I couldn't understand their language. Around every corner, I met people who wanted to tell me their story, and I am grateful to have been able to hear them.

I WAS ASSIGNED TO photograph the heroic work being done by the Azad India Foundation, an NGO that began in 1998 with a mission to provide job training to women in a single small village. Today, the organization has expanded to promote female literacy, broader job training and community health projects across the state, while developing a national voice on education and human rights. They understand the issues better than most: Bihar, for at least several decades, ranks among the lowest in India for social and economic development. With a total literacy rate of 63 percent (73 for men, but only 53 for women), it is the least literate state in the entire country.

The silver lining is how that situation has inspired people to join and found organizations like Azad, which is transforming people's lives through education.

This assignment was different from my others, however. The NGO's founder is a woman named Yuman Hussain, and while she's very influential in her community—along with her husband, a politician named Mohammad Jawaid—she was scheduled for a lengthy trip to Delhi the day after I arrived. So most of my interactions would be with my daily drivers, few of whom spoke English. Unlike my time in Botswana or Guatemala, I wouldn't have a direct office contact.

During my two-week assignment, my mornings always began at my hotel, when one of the foundation's coordinators would arrive with a warm greeting and a new assignment. From my hotel, I'd hop on the back of their motorcycles to ride at least 30 miles to different villages outside Kishanganj. Nearly every day, my driver was someone different, but all of them were caring, professional and safe—which is impressive, because anyone who's visited India knows how hectic the drives can be. We dodged cars and weaved through traffic, across small towns and the lush countryside, beeping our horn all the way. Whenever I needed something or felt unsafe, most of my drivers understood, despite the language barrier. We were speaking our own language, using only our eyes and gestures. The adventure of trying to communicate with locals was almost as thrilling as the rides themselves.

Inevitably, as is always the case when traveling, I had to place my trust wholeheartedly with a stranger. But it's important to feel uncomfortable sometimes, because it shakes us out of our everyday presumptions and mindsets.

This feeling was most prominent on my second morning, when I noticed from my hotel window that the fog outside was so thick I couldn't see more than a few feet. When my driver Taslim arrived, I tried to kill some time by sipping my tea slowly, hoping the fog would lift a bit before our long drive began. But I couldn't hold out forever, and eventually we had to leave, even though the haze hadn't cleared at all. There was not a glimpse of sunlight in sight. If Taslim spoke better English, I probably would have articulated my concerns about riding in those conditions—especially with my tricky lower back carrying all my camera equipment. But I couldn't tell him, and he seemed confident, so rather than waste more time trying to mime out my fears, I kept my mouth shut, tightened my backpack straps, took a few deep breaths, jumped on and placed my life in the hands of a complete stranger.

What happened over the next few hours was surreal, horrifying and magical. Honestly, it struck me almost like a religious experience.

We began our ride literally unable to see anything more than a foot ahead of the front tire; it was like being inside a thick cloud. Constant condensation lingered on the face guard of my helmet, and I compulsively wiped it clear with the sleeves of my shirt every five seconds, even though I couldn't see any better when I did.

I caught glimpses of local life: women steering cattle, lost chickens, stray dogs, men walking to work, a little boy herding goats, bicycles strapped with tall grass and bamboo, jam-packed tuk-tuks, speeding motorcyclists and even the rare sight of a car.

All this popped into view before vanishing just as quickly, like a child's flip-book unfolding beyond my control.

That morning, I saw everything that is important in the world. Faced with fear and reflection, I saw myself in every human and animal; in nature, the mist and the earth. I knew who I was, and that real life is pure love and full of light. Though I keep trying to write it down, no words can accurately describe it. The word that comes to mind, whenever I think about that long drive, is "peace."

Rarely do we get this chance to view snapshots of people's real lives, so briefly and in isolation. It gives us an opportunity to see ourselves in other people and things without judgment, to empathize and connect as members of a shared human race. We are all the same. We share the same hopes and dreams for ourselves and our families, the same basic needs, survival instincts and anxieties. I realized this during that foggy ride.

As a young man, I was naive and fearless, but as I grew older, I became scared of things. Scared of public speaking and embarrassment, scared of heights and pain. I have a fear of not being confident enough to say the right words and being judged by others, when I know I'll never be able to convey what I'm really thinking, who I really am. I think we all worry about this, at least sometimes. But after riding on the back of that motorcycle in a foggy, foreign place, I realized I had the ability overcome those insecurities. As Franklin D. Roosevelt famously said, "The only thing we have to fear is fear itself." What is there to be afraid of? These people lead much harder lives than I do, and yet they still manage to smile and greet strangers at their doorsteps. Public speaking is nothing next to the existential threat of flooding.

The fog did lift eventually as we approached the first village to visit some of the Azad Learning Centers that dotted the area. A photographer in a new foreign town is like a kid in a candy shop, and I immediately wanted to shoot every river, person and plant I saw. So full of renewed life and energy, I wanted to jump off the bike, run around the village and barge into the learning centers and just start shooting already. But I couldn't: I had to be patient, respectful and gain people's trust. They had stories they wanted me to hear, so first I had to listen.

My work turned out better as a result of this. I feel like the photographs I took were given to me, and not stolen in any way. These were not surreptitious street shots, but delicate portraits of people who graciously invited me into their lives. They wanted me to be there as much as I did. They were completely open, raw and willing to show me all the positive and negative aspects of their lives.

In the era of Instagram, anyone can snap a photo that might ricochet across the world. It's easy to believe that nothing on this planet has been left unseen. But these little pockets, these areas of innocence, where tourists don't go and even governments leave behind, are still out there, waiting to connect with the outside world. Many locals told me I was the first foreigner they had ever met. It was a lot of pressure, to be an ambassador for foreigners everywhere, but I hope I represented us well.

LIFE MAY BE HARD FOR many people in Bihar, but not once did anyone show a moment of unhappiness—only dignity for themselves and their communities. Every doorway was open for me, and within them I found nothing but genuine smiles and greetings of "Good morning, sir" (even if it was late afternoon). Often, locals would welcome me by bringing out a plastic chair to sit on, because that seemed to be all they had to offer a guest. It is customary to remove your shoes before entering most buildings in India, and I couldn't help but notice how dirty some of the kids' feet were—how difficult life must be at home, how far they may have walked to get to the center.

Every day, for nearly two weeks, I visited a variety of help centers for women's health and job training, computer labs for teens, extracurricular classes for children, family gatherings and income-generating workshops for gigs like sewing. One afternoon, I was invited to visit two participants from the sewing program at their homes, to see how the workshop helped them start their own businesses. That was one of the most rewarding parts of my assignment.

One woman I photographed was named Bilkis Begum. She received a sewing machine from the foundation in 2016, and two years later married a fellow tailor. She earned enough money to support her sister's education, and now works with her husband to earn around 10,000 rupees per month—about $130 in U.S. dollars—which is better than many people in this region, though still below the national average. Dressed in an electric-yellow sari, Bilkis demonstrated her daily work for me on her front porch, with the machine set up against the lime green wall of her home. Her neighbors gathered around us, watching in pride as she demonstrated her skill with a smile on her face.

It was refreshing to visit these local homes, because many of the Azad Foundation classrooms were dark and chilly, as electricity isn't reliably available in this part of India. The condition of the classes kept me on my toes, as I constantly tweaked my camera settings to squeeze out every ray of light available, which usually came from an open doorway or a single window in the back of a room. Because most mornings were chilly, the children all wore colorful layers of clothing and scarfs, which—mixed with the unusually textured walls and dim lighting—gave my images a striking vibrancy.

Most of my visits only lasted about 30 minutes, so I had to work quickly to find the best angles and lighting before being whisked off to the next location. Many times after the classroom work was done, the teachers gathered the children outside to lead them in different activities, which I always enjoyed photographing. I found myself interested in more than just the students and participants—in many locations, the village elders would watch from the outside, and they became part of the story. Once, during an activity outside, a local man walked over and sat down right in the middle of the field of children and seemed to start praying.

Visiting this region, and hearing these people's stories, ranks among the greatest privileges of my life. I am taking away a piece of kindness given to me and will now try to pass it on. I learned to be still and listen, and that the human spirit is fundamentally irrepressible, even in hard times. I understood the power of optimism and opportunity: there truly is something in this world for all of us to accomplish. The energy I picked up on that early foggy morning helped provide me with an unconditional faith in life and love. Even though I wasn't driving that motorcycle, I felt in control.

Close your eyes sometime, and just listen. You might be astonished at what emerges from the fog.

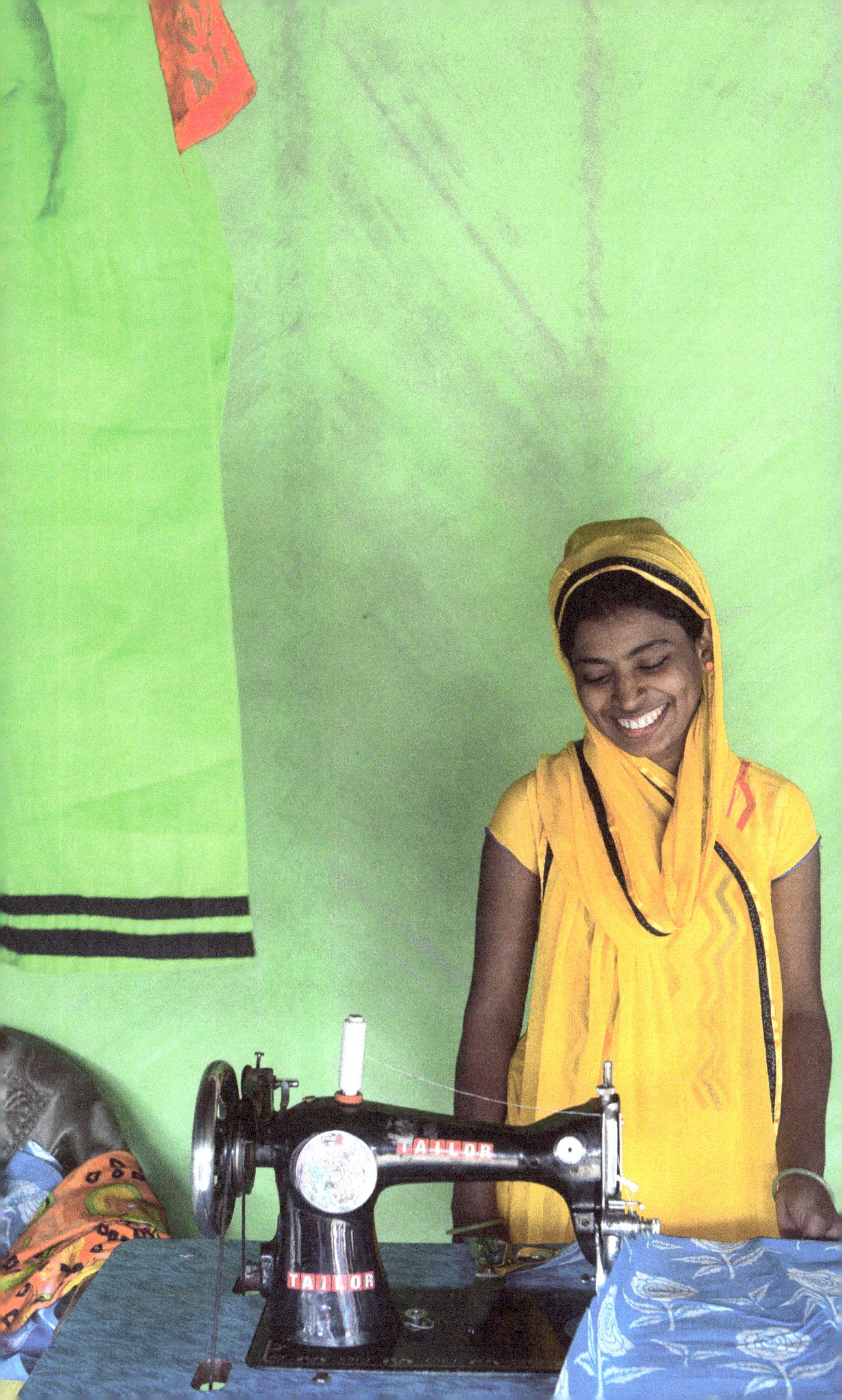
TAILOR
TAILOR

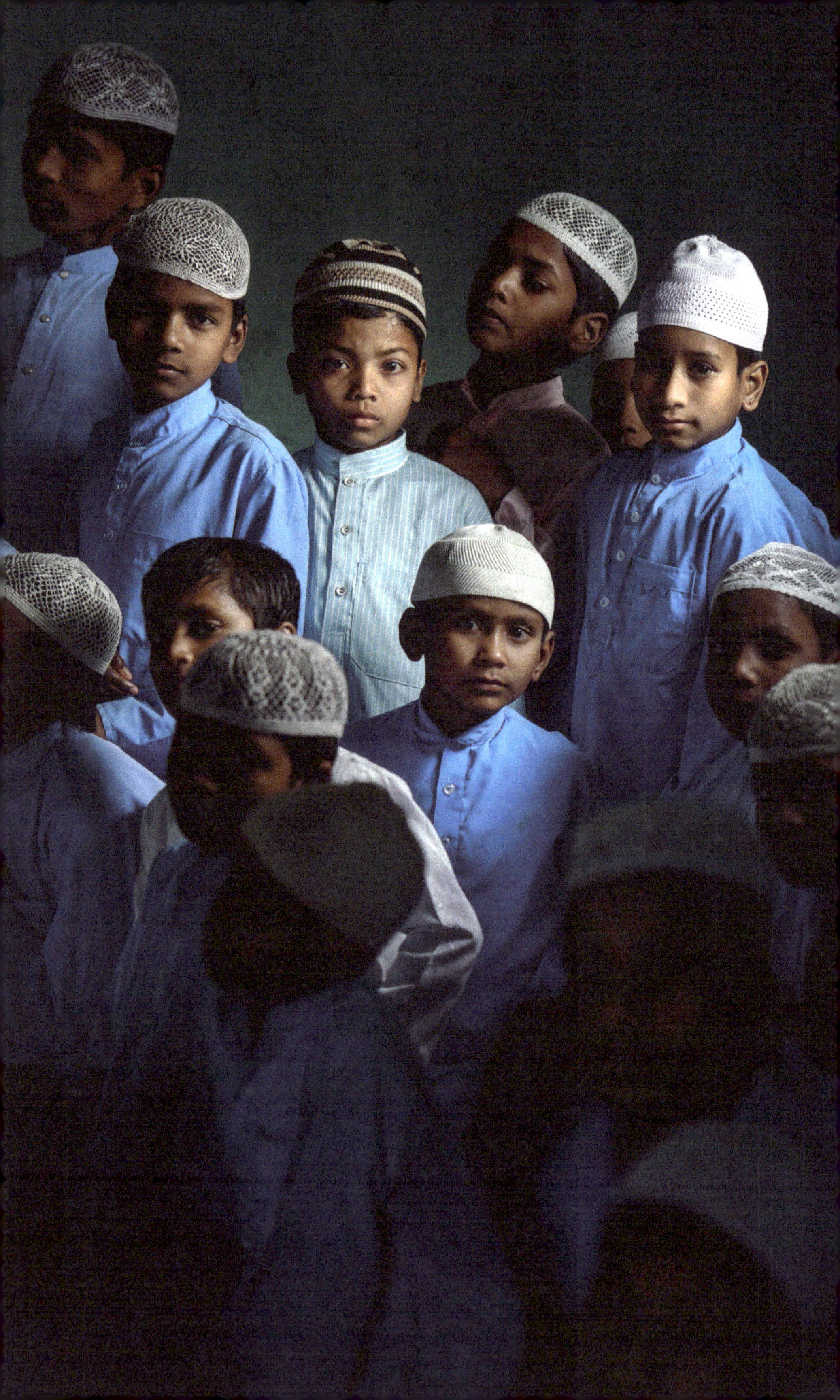

PHOTO TIP: FINDING THE LIGHT

Even when you can't see clearly in front of you, it's critical to find where the light is coming from. The best photographers know how to master light, how to manipulate it to illuminate their subjects in a certain way.

For beginners, I recommend a simple test to understand how light functions: shoot one single subject in every lighting condition you can. Shoot it right at sunrise and later during morning light; shoot it again in the afternoon and evening; shoot it at sunset, with moonlight, on a cloudy day, in the rain or snow. Shoot it inside with artificial light, like a flashlight or regular lamp. Compare all these images. Which one looks the best to you? There isn't always a right answer—it's about the emotion you're trying to convey. That's the first step to developing a personal style.

If you can understand, on a gut level, how to control light, and the ways light can affect your images, you can master another technique in telling a story within a photograph. Plenty of photographers are good at composition and Photoshop; it's a whole other challenge to master light. It's almost like speaking a secret language.

Whenever possible, I opt for natural light—any source not explicitly supplied by the photographer. The term "natural light" usually refers to sources of light that are beyond the artist's control, like the sun or moon, or pre-existing light that's already in the room.

I prefer natural light for a few reasons. Firstly, it's much easier to work with—no lugging around soft boxes, flashes or any extra gear. That makes it easier physically (it's always better to carry less weight), but also easier when shooting, because I can adjust my camera to whatever light already exists, rather than worrying about setting up a new rig.

Secondly, I find natural light more "true" to the image. Maybe it's my photojournalism background, but when I see something out in the world—whether it's a Guatemalan boy playing in a harshly sunlit street, a Ukrainian couple in an overcast forest or a turbaned man sipping tea in the shade of a Moroccan adobe house—you are given that light for a reason. Wandering the streets of Kishanganj, I would stage my photos only insofar as I needed my subjects to be clear and visible. But the clouds, sun and light naturally bouncing off the walls did all the rest.

The third reason I usually choose natural light may simply be that I'm so used to it. I've spent nearly 30 years as a photojournalist and travel photographer. Artificial light just isn't part of that genre. Natural light was foundational to how I learned photography. I'm used to it. So even if I'm shooting a wedding, I prefer to use natural light.

A single natural light source can be flexible, too. I'll give you an example. When I'm photographing a bride getting ready before the ceremony, I can photograph her near a window from inside the room and expose for the light streaming in, creating a silhouette of her. This is especially useful if the mother or bridesmaids are helping zip up her dress—I can keep them all backlit. After that, I might move toward the window with my back against it, and use that same natural window light to photograph a portrait of her front-lit. Then I might ask the bride to turn sideways, so her shoulder is closest to the window, and use a reflector on the opposite side of her. This catches that window light and bounces it back onto the dark side, creating a more fully lit image.

These are three examples of using the exact same light source—the sun and a single window—to create three completely different looks.

When working outdoors, my favorite way to use natural light is to pose the subject with their backs to the light (such as a setting sun) and fill in the front, darker side with a white or silver reflector. The strong backlight creates a dramatic effect, outlining the subjects with a warm glow and hair light (that's light that illuminates someone's hair), while the reflected light from the front softly fills in the dark shadows and provides a small catch light in the subject's eyes.

When natural light is unavailable, it's almost impossible to get a well-exposed photograph without introducing some type of artificial light, such as a flash, strobe or video light. The trick here is to try and emulate a natural light source (such as the sun) as much as you can. I try to light these types of assignments with off-camera lighting. ("Off-camera lighting" refers to light that isn't attached to the camera itself—think of a studio setup, rather than an external flash connected atop the camera body.)

I typically use a long off-camera cord that stretches from the hot shoe to the flash, or a trigger that sends a signal to from the camera to a flash or strobe that is out of the frame on a light stand. It's essential to use some type of diffuser, such as a soft-box or umbrella for most portraits, which effectively softens and redirects the light source into a broader, more aesthetically pleasing source of light.

I also use a tiny video LED light to provide small highlights in some of my images, which is a quick way to balance what light is already available with a small, unobtrusive light source.

Regardless of your light source, you'll want a light meter to know exactly how well exposed your image is. When shooting with a digital camera, I feel pretty confident using the in-camera light meter to discern the correct exposure, although I still whip out my trusty handheld Sekonic light meter when I'm shooting film or chrome slides.

Light meters read the light in different ways, but there are two basic techniques. One method measures the light reflecting off the subject, and the other takes an incident reading by measuring the light as it falls on the subject. There are several ways to achieve a variety of effects with my lighting techniques depending on what is available (naturally or in my camera bag) and the feeling I am trying to create.

Light is the great secret to photography. But understanding it is like learning a musical instrument: it requires practice, patience and experimentation. With enough time, you'll understand it naturally. Once that happens, you'll unlock a great tool for storytelling. You'll be able to catch the light in someone's eyes and the color in their clothes. You'll be better equipped to tell their story, because you'll be better able to see them clearly.

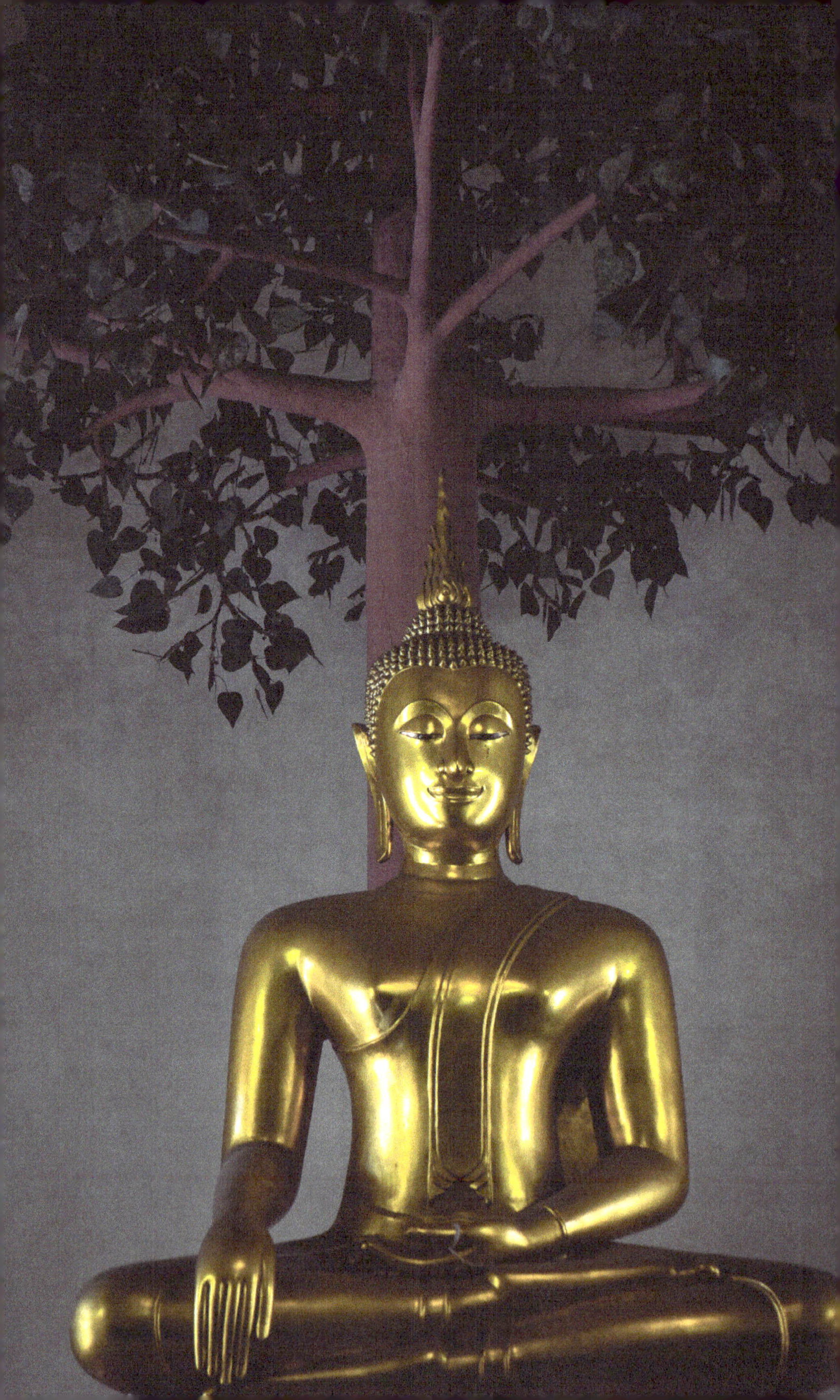

CHAPTER 7

SERENDIPITY IN THE TROPICS

"Man cannot discover new oceans unless he has the courage to lose sight of the shore."

– Andre Gide

I've been fascinated by the "digital nomad" phenomenon for a few years now. As a photographer, my job is pretty mobile. Even though I specialize in weddings from my home in Florida, I've been lucky to have my photography take me around the world, both to shoot destination weddings and other assignments.

I've never committed full-time to the digital nomad life, though I do split my time these days between the United States and Peru. Because I spend so much time in that continental transition, a few years ago, I went through a period of scouring YouTube videos and blog posts on how to make more money while living a semi-nomadic life. In my research, I learned about something called the Nomad Summit in Chiang Mai, a popular digital nomad hot spot in Northern Thailand.

My partner and I watched a few videos together when we

learned about it, and kind of half-jokingly promised to go someday. I had always been curious about Thailand, but it wasn't at the top of my bucket list.

A few months later, I got word that I'd be traveling to India for Photographers Without Borders. When I looked up the region I'd be heading to—a state called Bihar, in India's northeast—I couldn't help but notice how close Thailand was.

Okay, sure, Bangkok was still around 2,000 miles away from Bihar. But that's a heck of a lot closer than it is to New York. And when I double-checked the Nomad Summit website, I was shocked to find that the conference was being held the same month I'd be in India.

Could I actually make this happen?

Obviously my India assignment took priority, so I had to wait a few weeks before finalizing my itinerary. But once those dates were set, I realized it was a real possibility to attend the summit. My partner took a little convincing, but eventually we were on the same page, and before we knew it, we were boarding our Emirates flight from Fort Lauderdale to Bangkok via Dubai.

After nearly 40 hours of traveling, we hopped into an Uber to Bangkok's upscale Silom district, where our apartment-style hotel, Park Saladaeng, awaited us. The rooms were small but nicely furnished, and we agreed it was the perfect place to catch up on sleep before exploring the so-called "Big Mango." (Like the Big Apple, but Bangkok-style.)

On our first day in the city, we were pleasantly surprised by how inexpensive things were. Transportation was very affordable, and most of the 90-minute massages—available on every street corner—were less than $15. (We partook almost every day, thank you very much.) Hefty portions of bouncy fried rice and oily pad Thai rarely cost more than four bucks. Plus, the Thai people, famous for their hospitality, were all gracious and friendly to us, and the local attractions were world-class, just like the travel guides promised.

Bangkok acts as a sort of regional capital for all of Southeast Asia and is a common starting point for the "Banana Pancake Trail." The trail is a loop around Southeast Asia that's very popular among backpackers and digital nomads. It takes you from Bangkok to Siem Reap and Phnom Penh in Cambodia; across to Ho Chi Minh City in Vietnam; up along the rocky Vietnamese coast to Hot An, Hue and Hanoi; into foggy mountains surrounding Luang Prabang in Laos; and, finally, across the snaking Mekong River to Chiang Mai, in the northern jungles of Thailand. Most trips take a couple weeks (if not months), and Bangkok is usually the starting and ending point, since its airport is a major international hub.

We weren't prepared to do all that, but suffice it to say, Bangkok's tourist infrastructure is rock-solid. The areas around the city are often super crowded, and with good reason: the titanic golden Buddha statues, towering stupas and vibrant gemstones adorning every temple are a marvel to behold.

We visited many of these sites, such as Wat Pho, with its famously massive reclining Buddha (150 feet long and 15 feet tall); Wat Arun, an intricately designed riverside temple decorated with white porcelain; and the famous Royal Palace, a complex so big we could never see it all in a single visit. We also enjoyed a quick boat ride, which took us around the floating markets of Damnoen Saduak, west of the city. Vendors there sell their wares on longboats floating in the region's ubiquitous canals. The water may not be clean, but the sight is unforgettable.

After three days and two nights in the capital city, it was time to head north. We stopped for a night in Ayutthaya, which was once the region's capital when this was the Ayutthayan Empire. (After that empire crumbled in the 18th century, Siam rose to power.) Ayutthaya lies about 50 miles north of Bangkok—a short 90-minute train ride that cost less than $5. We stayed at a reasonably priced hotel in the city center and enjoyed walking through the local day market—and, of course, getting a massage on our first day.

We woke up early on our second day to try and make it to Wat Chaiwatthanaram before sunrise. Although it officially doesn't open until 8 a.m., I was able to snag some beautiful photos from outside. The Khmer-style temples, built by the king in the 17th century to honor his mother, were stunning, and watching the rising sun flare up between the stupas was a wonderful gift to photograph.

The entire temple complex exists within the old city of Ayutthaya, which is actually an island. We managed to see the discolored stone temples of Wat Phra Si Sanphet and the large stone Buddha heads of Wat Ratchaburana. While tourism is definitely a lynchpin of this city, there weren't nearly as many tourists there as there were in Bangkok, which makes recommending this city a no-brainer.

After a full day of sightseeing, it was time to return to our hotel to pack up for our overnight train ride to Chiang Mai. We hadn't planned any of our trip ahead of time, preferring to travel spontaneously. Unfortunately, we'd have done well to plan some things ahead: I read online that two overnight trains had sleeper cars, and that the tickets were less expensive if bought at the station instead of online. But once we arrived at the station, we were told that both trains were totally full—the curse of traveling during the high season. The only train with any seats available left at 11 p.m., but it was composed entirely of third-class cars—meaning the only seats were hard benches with minimal cushioning.

It was definitely not the romantic train ride I'd envisioned, but what can you do? We sat upright, awake and uncomfortable for most of our 13-hour overnight ride. The upside is that we got to meet more Thai people this way, exchanging eye contact and smiles. We rode the cheapest, least comfortable train like true locals, rather than merely sleeping in privacy and comfort. Privacy and comfort are overrated, anyway!

Okay, I might be over-compensating a little, but the trip was honestly not that bad, and became one of the most memorable moments of my time in Thailand. The views from the train's large windows, chugging through rural farm towns and vast mountains as the sun peaked in the east, were so impressive I wanted to stay awake even after a rough sleep.

Needless to say, once we arrived in Chiang Mai at noon, we beelined for our hotel, called the RCN Court and Inn, located in the center of the Old City, for a belated night's rest. Booking a quality hotel for $35 a night turned out to be the best investment we made that trip, and our bodies thanked us for it.

The Nomad Summit kicked off the next day, promptly at 9 a.m. at Le Meridien Hotel. Hundreds of travelers from around the world were here, and we listened to a few prominent entrepreneurs, digital marketers, roaming artists and business experts. I was especially interested in Johnny FD, who organized the whole event, and turned out to be very approachable and a captivating speaker. We also appreciated hearing what Matt Bowles had to say about real estate, since we had firsthand experience running our own little bed and breakfast in Peru.

After a whole day of knowledge-gathering and business

planning, the day's events concluded with an after-party on the roof of the Maya Mall, which boasted terrific views of the city. The party was a great place to network with the day's speakers and our fellow attendees, and also meet some popular digital nomads we'd seen on YouTube, like Riley from *Living That Life*. It was startling to be meeting in person so many influencers we'd only known through our computer screens a few months before.

We booked a few extra days in Chiang Mai to explore, of course. Aside from our daily massages, we enjoyed walking the streets of the Old City, meeting new people and eating terrific Thai food. We also managed to fit in a trip outside the city limits to an elephant sanctuary where visitors can learn about these tremendous creatures, feed them, and walk alongside them. Elephant tourism is tricky to navigate in Thailand, and many so-called "sanctuaries" operate highly unethically. This one was good, as it didn't allow elephant riding (which is an abusive practice.) The grounds were a little small for the 15 or so elephants living there, but you could tell the staff really cared about them, and we loved being able to prepare their food and walk alongside them in harmony.

One of the best parts of my trip to Thailand, however, may not have had to do with Thailand at all. By bizarre happenstance, while vacationing in one tropical country, I was lucky enough to win an all-expenses-paid trip to another, whole oceans away: I was off to Brazil.

THE BEAUTIFUL BRAZILIAN island of Florianópolis is more than 10,000 miles away from Chiang Mai, but the two tropical destinations share much by way of beauty, warmth and accommodations. The whole island of Florianópolis is a single city of more than one million people, with excellent quality of life boosted by tourism and IT industries. The city's climate is gorgeous, with record-high temperatures barely cracking 100 degrees Fahrenheit.

All these factors have made Florianópolis one of the best places to live in Brazil. It's not even just the locals who say so: *The New York Times* crowned it the "Party Destination of the Year" in 2009; *Newsweek* ranked it one of the 10 "most dynamic cities of the world" in 2006. A local Brazilian publication called *Veja* outright dubbed it the best place to live in the entire country. This attention has transformed the city into an attractive hot spot for tourists, expats and locals alike, all of whom are drawn in by the sunny climate and the beautiful beaches.

I hadn't heard of it before visiting, but serendipity struck. During the Nomad Summit, I entered one of those social media contests where you have to like and comment on someone's post to enter a raffle. The contest was held by a guy named Mike LaRosa, whose company, Coworkaholic, connects travelers with shared workspaces across the world. I entered the contest as soon as I heard about it, and the next morning, Mike messaged me that I'd won.

My trip included a stay at a “personal growth retreat center” called Rosemary Dream. Located in Barra da Lagoa, a traditional fishing village, Rosemary is surrounded by jungle and is a quick walk to the ocean, giving it the perfect balance of natural wonders.

If you’re considering a visit, though, know that the owners play up this connection to nature pretty hard. Rosemary is not a place for people who aren’t into the modern hippy, healthy, invigorating, transformative, organic aesthetic that’s so common among rustic-chic accommodations these days. It’s a sleekly contemporary space, but the mosquito nets and shared cabins remind you that you’re still mere steps away from the Brazilian wilderness.

Rosemary focuses on personal empowerment, workshops and events that shake out everyday drudgery from its visitors. There’s a whole range of facilities, including a wide wooden deck for meditation and yoga, and a lush botanical garden overlooking a lake. Step out the back door and you’ll walk right into the jungle; turn to the right and you’ll be at the beach in two minutes.

For me, the center was unbelievably relaxing, and truly helped rejuvenate me with meditation courses and vegan meals. The staff went above and beyond to ensure my comfort, and the optional mosquito net—in case I wanted to sleep with the window open at night—was a nice touch.

Beyond the lodge’s walls, Florianópolis struck me as colorful and upbeat, with plenty of street art and architecture. The blend struck me as both proud and challenging of its country—indeed, there is good reason for both.

Where an ocean is, surfers flock. I saw a countless surfers in Florianópolis, and some—presumably locals—were very skilled at the sport. They rode the waves like they had been doing it since birth. The medium-sized waves were perfect for surfing, and so was the hot and sunny weather.

The view of the city is just as lovely as actually being inside of it. All the houses are colorful and bright, and the natural surroundings cast a perfect backdrop. A verdant green mountain slopes down into the urban landscape, popping up lazily beside the city.

The food was also amazing. Fresh seafood was on almost every menu, and I found it hard to resist—despite the island's technological transformation, it remains inhabited by many fishermen who rely on a fresh catch from the ocean every day. One morning I saw a boy holding a fish and looking down at it with an expression I could only describe as wonder. Many locals understand that they live in harmony with wildlife, as it surrounds them on all sides.

Every morning, I ate with chopsticks alongside my morning coffee with a beautiful view from a lovely balcony. The air was fresh with the scent of a beach breeze, and that alone could have refreshed my senses. It was an unexpected trip—certainly not one

I'd planned—but then again, so was my excursion to Thailand until a few months earlier, and that one only came together because of a separate trip to India. Serendipity exists all around us. All you have to do is open yourself up to the possibilities.

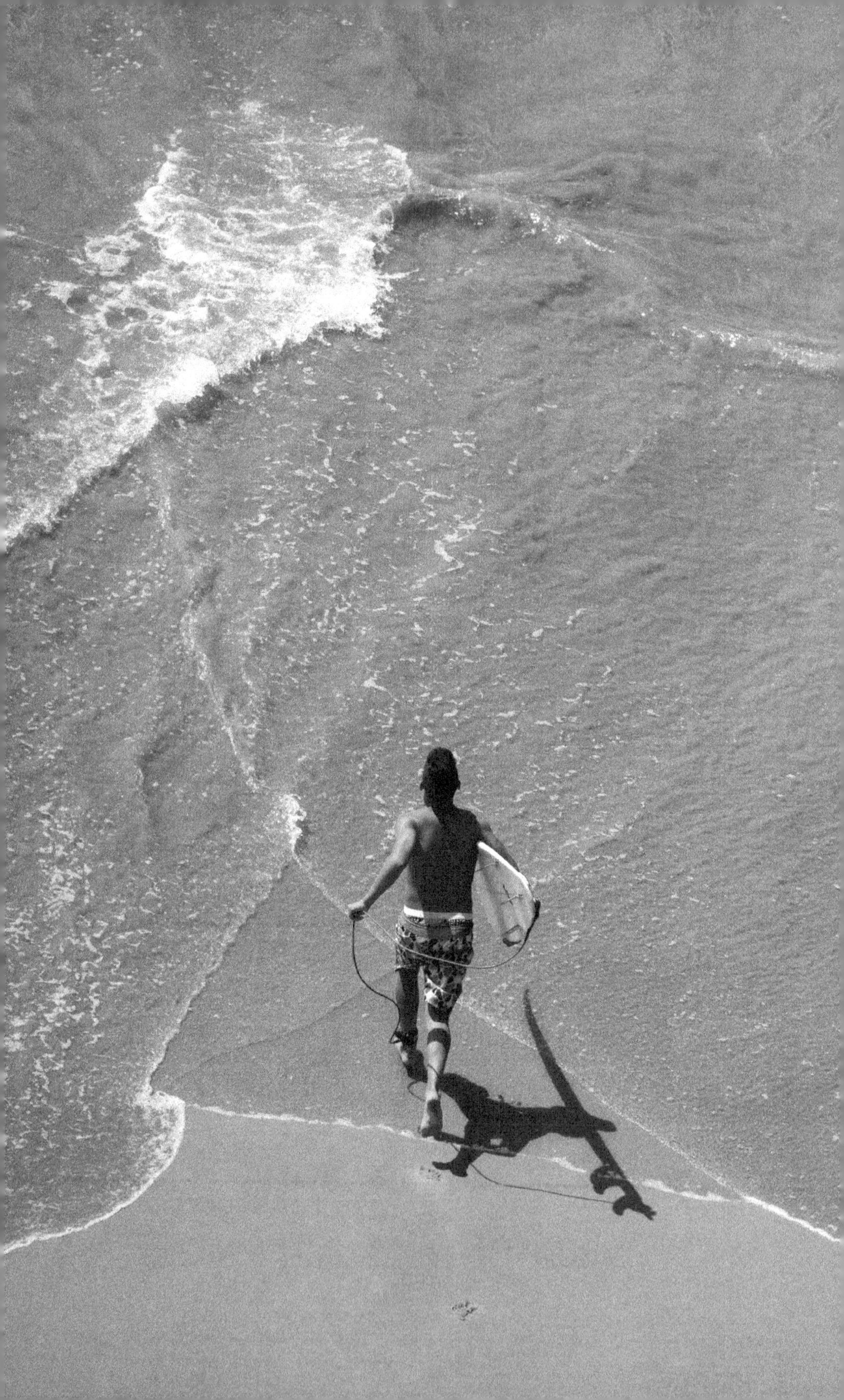

PHOTO TIP: WHEN TO EDIT—AND WHEN TO NOT

If you aren't familiar with my magazine, you can find it on my blog, *artstyleflow.com*. It's finally given me the opportunity to feature my travel and fashion photography the way a graphic designer would—and it's only because I'm familiar with the Adobe suite of photo-editing software.

Adobe has become the worldwide standard for photographic post-production, and it's my go-to default as well. I first learned to use Adobe Photoshop in 1994, using version 2.5 on an Apple Macintosh LC 500. At the time, it was very exciting for us students at the art institute to get out of the darkroom—away from the enlarger, test strips, fixer chemicals—and into the computer lab.

Today, I own a sleek new 27-inch iMac, complete with the latest versions of Adobe Lightroom and Photoshop. I use them almost daily. It's a whole other world to see my work so up-close, noticing the depth and detail in millions of megapixels, and perfecting them using the best software available.

I shot film until about 2005 and was a little nervous making the switch to digital. But I can confidently say that digital imaging has far surpassed the days of film. Back in the '90s, when I first tinkered with Photoshop, I was bogged down by a lot of cutting, pasting and slowly carving outlines with the lasso tool. Today, between my years of practice and Adobe's upgrades, using layers and action tools can create vibrant, beautiful photographs extremely quickly.

I shoot all of my work in RAW format, sometimes dubbed a "digital negative," which has all the "uncooked" information. The default JPEG file type is much smaller but has already been processed a bit in the camera, so your images will have less information—basically, less detail. It makes it harder to edit.

The editing process is obviously fundamental to modern photography, and you've probably noticed this even if you're not into Photoshop. Every photographic app—even just the standard smartphone camera apps—feature some kind of quick post-production work, usually limited to cropping, brightness, contrast and saturation. Preset filters make this faster, though you give up control when you use them.

I prefer a conservative approach to editing, letting my composition and the image's natural light tell most of the story. But for those curious, I'll outline my post-production process a bit here, and offer a few tips and suggestions for how to optimize your time working with Adobe products.

Step one is always to back up all my photos multiple times, always on different external hard drives. Home organization of external hard drives is a whole other issue, but suffice it to say, if you're planning on being a pro photographer, you've either got to be incredibly well organized—or be prepared to spend a lot on cloud storage. I then load all the RAW files into Adobe Lightroom. Lightroom has similar functions to Photoshop, but they work in tandem. Lightroom cannot edit your photos, nor can it move your images to different places on your hard drive. Instead, all the changes you make are kept in a catalog, which is like a place for instructions on how each image should be processed. When you apply some type of adjustment, Lightroom is essentially keeping a log of the alterations in a database, while leaving the original image untouched. This is referred to as "nondestructive editing," which stands in contrast to how Photoshop works.

You can create your own presets in Lightroom or download a bunch of pre-made ones from professional editors—these are essentially filters. You can create a certain type of black-and-white preset, for example, and apply it in bulk to all your photos. I don't tend to do this, and I find most presets out there to be a little too trendy. Besides, if you ever needed to go back to an original version of their image, you'd need to reopen the RAW file in Lightroom and start over. But for some photographers, especially those who specialize in mobile photography, Lightroom accomplishes everything they need, and they might bypass Photoshop altogether. For Instagram, the end product is strong enough. For print, it's a different story.

I mostly use Lightroom to add keywords and metadata to all of my images in the import area of the program, and then sync several global adjustments to all of my photos in the develop mode, such as clarity, contrast, vibrancy, saturation, sharpening and a slight darkening of the edges to all the images (similar to a technique called "burning" I used to do in the darkroom). I like to keep my pictures pretty simple in Lightroom, without overworking them, so I have a good, well-exposed copy of the collection. Because you can tackle these edits in bulk, or at least shift between images more quickly, it speeds up the post-production process significantly. This is also great for someone like me, who much prefers to spend his professional time out in the field.

Once I export my final color-corrected, cropped selections as JPEGs, I usually do not go back into Lightroom with them. At this point, they're generally ready to go to the client, but if there is any more work needed on a photo, that's when I turn to Photoshop.

Photoshop is a much more intense software, with a steeper learning curve, that allows users to manipulate, crop, resize and color correct images. It's the standard-bearer for gauging white balance and ensuring black-and-white images have the correct amount of contrast, too.

The best way to start with Photoshop is to create what are called layers. Think of transparent films you slide over you photos, which you can edit however you like; if it doesn't look good, you can make the layer invisible. Working with layers keeps you from touching the original image, and instead give every adjustment its own space. That gives you greater flexibility with no serious drawbacks if you screw something up—just delete that layer and start fresh. Compounding layers, and seeing how different filters and edits work together, is part of the beauty of the system.

I personally don't get too involved with multiple layers, and instead primarily use Photoshop for a plugin called Portraiture. It does an outstanding job of smoothing people's skin for small blemishes and tends to give my photos an extra pop. For more creative work, such as senior portraits or fine-art photography, I have several texture overlays I apply using layers. This is to add an extra level of depth and quality to my images. Since my major in school was photojournalism, I prefer to present my photographs with a realistic publishable feel, which means minimizing the editing as much as possible. I like the natural textures, composition and lighting to speak for themselves.

I'm keenly aware of staying up-to-date with Adobe's annual updates, and I've found it incredibly helpful to attend workshops, conferences and other continuing-education meetings to keep current with its new abilities.

All things photography have changed immensely since my early days at the art institute computer lab. But in some ways, Adobe has done *too good* of a job with its products. I spend more time than

I'd like sitting at my desk, tweaking images like a perfectionist. It's easy to get sucked in for hours, days or even weeks working on a project that a professional lab would have handled quickly before the year 2000. But that's the story of technology, in many ways. When something good becomes popular, everyone flocks to it.

But the rise of digital editing, including one-click filters, hasn't done much to disrupt professional photography. Even serious hobbyists would be smart to move away from them. I find a lot of these filtered photos look too trendy, too much like a fleeting fad. Consider what people might say 10 years from now. Unless you have a very specific goal to create a certain mood that reflects our era, I suggest striving for timelessness. A classic look never goes out of style.

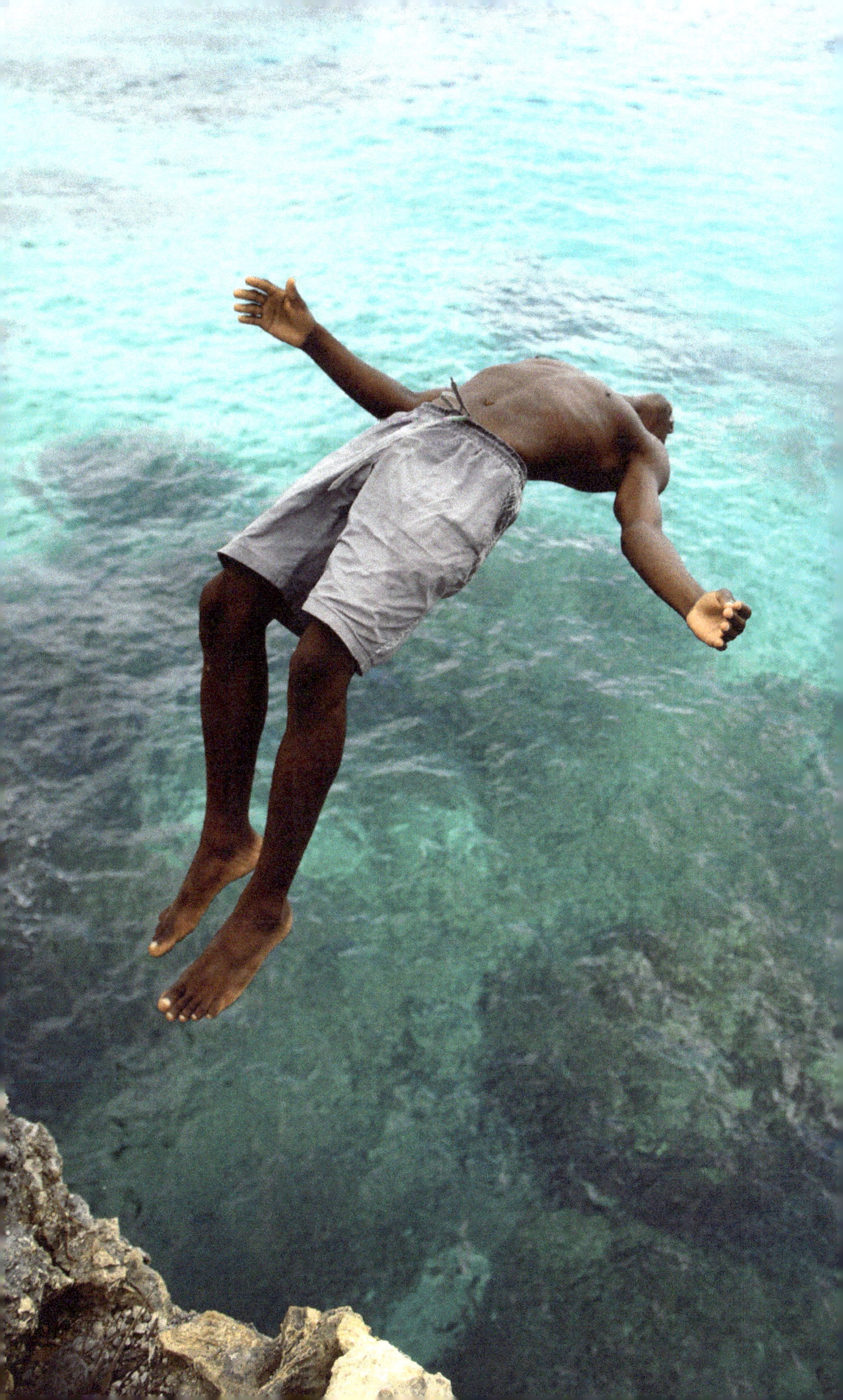

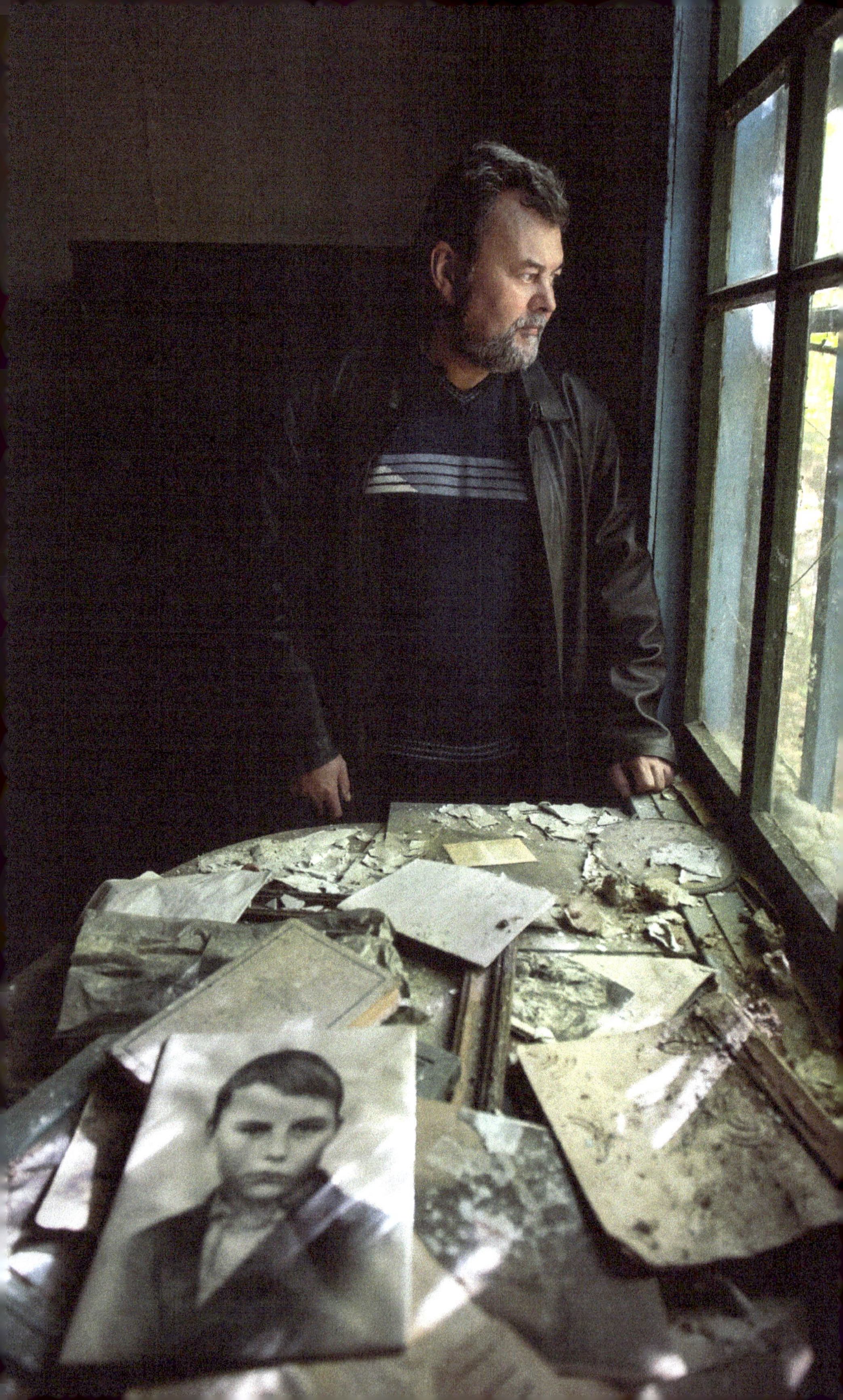

CHAPTER 8

THE FALLOUT IN CHERNOBYL

" 'Man,' I cried, 'how ignorant art thou in thy pride of wisdom!' "
– Mary Shelley, Frankenstein

I remember 1986 vividly. I was a typical teenager waiting tables for tips, saving money for college and travel. It cost less than dollar per gallon to fill my old Volkswagen Beetle, which was often blasting the latest songs by Madonna, my favorite singer. Oprah made her national debut that year, and *The Phantom Of The Opera* opened in London's West End, a few months after the public charity event "Hands Across America" raised $15 million to help those in poverty.

But some events linger in my memory more than others. The outbreak of Mad Cow Disease in England and the Space Shuttle Challenger tragedy piqued my interest, as I'd started keeping up with the news and becoming more aware of the world around me. But another global tragedy of 1986 is what totally absorbed me:

the explosion of reactor 4 at the Chernobyl nuclear power plant in Ukraine, at the time still part of the Soviet Union.

I clearly remember Peter Jennings reporting that little was known about the nuclear accident on ABC's *World News Tonight*. After seeing that initial report, I was glued to the TV for days, waiting for the slow trickle of information. The Soviets weren't keen to release more information than was necessary, but they may have been relatively quick to respond to this because evidence of nuclear radiation had already reached into Scandinavia and Central Europe.

At the time, Chernobyl was something of a showcase facility with an excellent safety record. It sat near the city of Kiev, with nearly three million inhabitants, about 1,000 miles from Scandinavia. Details were hazy at first, but the world quickly realized that whatever happened there lead to a radioactive cloud headed north over Poland, to Denmark, Finland, Norway and Sweden. It would turn out to be the most severe accident to ever take place in the short history of civil nuclear power.

Little news was being released initially from Chernobyl, even to the leaders in Moscow. In an interview years later, Mikhail Gorbachev, the leader of the Soviet Union at the time, said he was first alerted of the severity of the accident from Sweden. The world eventually learned that the radioactive fallout was many times greater than the combined power of the two nuclear bombs dropped on Hiroshima and Nagasaki during the Second World War.

I've remained intrigued by Chernobyl over the years. In 1997, while on a photojournalism internship in Budapest, I almost visited the Ukrainian disaster site to document how life had changed in the area in the decade since the explosion. But due to time constraints, I never made it. The newsreels and still images I'd seen from the accident would have to remain where they were: embedded in the back of my mind, categorized for some kind of future use.

IN 2018, I RECEIVED AN email from Maxx Kochar, the program manager from Photographers Without Borders. He had a special request for me, to see if I was interested in going to Ukraine to cover the story of an NGO called the Clean Futures Fund, which helps local communities in and around Chernobyl affected by the accident. It took me about two seconds to hit the "reply all" button with one simple word: "YES!"

I was on my way, representing PWB to cover all the heroic things the CFF is working on at Chernobyl. They have missions in Pripyat (the city built for the workers of the power plant) and Slavutych (a similar city built for displaced citizens after the accident), as well as goals to provide health care services for local survivors, liquidators who helped clean up the mess, orphanages, rehabilitation centers and a special project for animals.

Once the project was confirmed, I began brushing up on my knowledge of the accident and the progress made over the years, but I tried to limit myself to just the basics. I intentionally stayed away from recent photographs and videos, as I wanted to see for myself and to experience my honest emotions once I got there, without any expectations. How would being in a place like that feel? What could I learn there? Was our global idea of what Chernobyl is like be at all accurate?

Luckily for me, and for the project as a whole, Jeff Garriock, a Canadian filmmaker, was assigned by PWB as a documentarian to shoot a short film about Chernobyl and the CFF story. This was my fourth project for Photographers Without Borders, but my first one traveling with another storyteller. Once I arrived, I eagerly started brainstorming with Jeff. With his help, I was able to learn more about the full story behind my own images. He always asked smart, informative questions, without which I would have just been left to snap photographs of visually interesting things—then left on my own to do the research and craft the narrative.

Another person who proved invaluable to the process was the co-founder of the CFF and our host for 14 days in Ukraine, Lucas Hixson. From the moment I met Lucas at the airport, on our three-hour drive to Slavutych and during our entire time together, he never ceased to amaze me. He had more energy than anyone I'd ever met. He couldn't have slept more than three hours a night, yet he was always the first one awake, bouncing around with fresh ideas, fearlessly leading us on our daily adventures, drinking endless cups of "Caffè Americano," and he was always the last one to go to bed at night.

One evening, after a long day, I was ready to retire by about 9 p.m. I said goodnight, assuming everyone else was as exhausted as I was and would be right behind me. The next morning, at an early breakfast, I asked everyone how they slept. Lucas informed me that after I went off to bed, he and a friend visited a nearby vineyard to pick grapes until 1 a.m.

I have countless stories about him like that. He seemed to thrive on a small amount of rest, yet still managed to come up with new ways of doing things with laser focus. Not only was Lucas one of the most energetic and smartest people I'd met—his background is in nuclear science—but he also happened to be one of the funniest. One minute he could be discussing how uranium atoms split and the difference between alpha, beta and gamma radiation; a minute later he could quote classic *Saturday Night Live* skits verbatim. He truly is one of the most interesting people I'd ever met in my life, and I'm a better person for having worked so closely with him on this project.

His non-profit, the Clean Futures Fund, raises awareness about industrial accidents and offers support for the communities affected and the remediation workers whose job it is to clean the area up. The organization works with these on-the-ground forces directly, fundraising for projects to help workers live their best lives with accessible health care and education for their families, to compensate for the fact that they're risking themselves for the sake of our planet.

Lucas co-founded the CFF with Erik Kambarian in 2016, and it's amazing how much success they've had in just a few short years. They had visited Chernobyl several times even before starting the CFF and struck up friendships with numerous remediation workers whose job could take decades longer.

During my stay with them, we were kept very busy. In reality, I felt eager to learn as much as possible in a short amount of time; yet I somehow also felt like we spent a lifetime there. Our hosts, Lucas and Rita (whom Lucas describes as "the manager of everything"), could not have been more helpful, professional and inspiring.

Our primary goal as documentarians and storytellers was to tie the Chernobyl power plant and Pripyat, the city evacuated and abandoned after the nuclear accident, together with the current life in Slavutych. Both cities were built for and around the workers of Chernobyl. We had our plan.

Before arriving, I thought we would spend most of our time in Slavutych, but we visited Chernobyl and Pripyat almost every day. Getting to the plant was a smooth 45-minute train ride from our home base in Slavutych. There were three morning trains, departing at 7:20, 7:40 and 10 a.m. Workers would wait on the train platform drinking coffee, shaking hands, chatting and smoking one last cigarette before boarding the train at the very last possible moment. Interestingly, most of our ride took us through the country of Belarus, across a dimple of land emerging from its southern border. Even though the train never stops in Belarus, it was important to carry our passports with us, just in case.

Being there in October was the perfect time to visit, as the changing colors of the trees made for a beautiful sight, both on the train ride and in the surrounding villages. I could spend hours watching the plant workers pass time on the train. Some sleepily stared out the window the entire trip; others tried to rest as their heads bobbed back and forth; a few played cards as seriously as a game of high-stakes poker.

I'll never forget our first day on the train, and the moment that power plant came into view. Between the thin, vaguely mystical fog and the abundance of trees, I could only catch glimpses of the plant itself, but I knew it was there: the crumbling old facade of Chernobyl mixed with the New Safe Confinement structure, dubbed "the Arch," which covers the site of reactor 4. I'd seen some photos and watched a few old documentaries, but nothing quite prepared me for being there in person.

There it was, the doorstep of the world's worst nuclear accident. And I was about to walk inside.

ON OUR FIRST DAY AT Chernobyl, we ventured inside the exclusion zone. The Soviet government set up the 19-mile-radius restricted area shortly after the explosion, blocking off anything and anyone from getting close to the nuclear fallout. Over the years, the borders have expanded to cover a larger swath of the country, giving remediation crews, scientists and ecologists the freedom to work in the area comprehensively.

It was fascinating to stand within those borders and witness the daily life of workers passing through a series of checkpoints, jumping on buses and heading off to work in such a surreal environment.

But we wouldn't actually enter the plant yet. First, we were off to visit Pripyat.

Pripyat, named after the nearby Pripyat River, is a ghost town today. It was founded in 1970 and built to serve the people of the power plant, less than two miles away. By the time of the disaster, the town was home to nearly 50,000 people.

It's said to be a city looking to the future, now tragically locked in the past. The local government oversaw the construction of many schools, a large hospital complex, stores, gyms, huge parks, cinemas, factories, a vast cultural center, an amusement park and other landmarks of a thriving community.

At the time, Pripyat was one of the most beautiful, modern cities in the Soviet Union. Over three decades later, the town is now a freeze-frame of 1986. Communist propaganda still hangs on its crumbling walls; personal belongings litter the streets and abandoned buildings. The iconic Soviet hammer and sickle still adorns its walls, as if awaiting a May Day celebration that will never happen. Toys, books and school supplies can be seen around a schoolhouse, where they were last played with and left behind by children who are now fully grown—if still alive.

I was shocked by each place I visited, because I didn't know what to anticipate. Rather than full of despair, I saw these places as stunning and peaceful. It was actually lovely to see the way nature had begun reclaiming its territory. Yes, some of Pripyat is eerie, but it's never alarming—you don't feel unsafe walking down its streets. Of course, I tried to remain mindful that nothing is really "safe" in the exclusion zone: there are giant holes in the floor, nails poking out of random beams and shards of broken glass blanketing the ground, not to mention the radioactive dust covering almost everything. Nonetheless, it was liberating to freely explore this abandoned and decaying city.

The only sadness I felt was when I wondered how long the town might be around for, before it gets demolished or degrades entirely. In its own way, Pripyat is beautiful.

ONE DAY, WE HAD THE privilege of meeting a man named Ivan and his wife, Olena. Both lived in the area before the accident, and neither had been able to visit since. Ivan grew up in a small village called Kopachi, outside Chernobyl; he later moved to Pripyat, where he lived in an apartment. Olena rented a separate apartment in Pripyat while they were dating. We decided to visit all three locations—the first time any of them had been to these places in over 30 years.

The problem was, Ivan didn't remember how to reach his childhood home. We drove to the closest location he could remember, though none of us knew exactly what we were looking for; to make matters worse, most roads were now covered with waist-high (and even sometimes neck-high) bushes, trees and weeds. There were no street signs or landmarks left to guide us. We considered giving up at one point, simply conducting our interview and photo shoot in an old barn overgrown with flora that we chanced upon.

But Ivan wanted to push forward, and so we did, continuing into the unfamiliar. Along the way, stopping for an occasional cigarette, Ivan told us some stories about being a kid, how he'd swim with other children in a stream that's now arid dirt. But he was most excited to share a story about a large oak tree in his front yard, which he used to play under and climb. This seemed to be one of his fondest memories and may well be what fueled his drive to venture onward with us that afternoon.

After hours of navigating the region, we could tell by the look on Ivan's face that he finally remembered his way home.

Jeff, Lucas, Rita and I had fallen a few steps behind Ivan and Olena, but when we saw them begin to speed up, we dashed ahead just in time to see Ivan embrace a massive oak tree that stood tall and mighty in his old front yard. Holding on tight, he gazed up with pride, a blissful smile and a tear in his eye. This was it: this was home.

What happened next could not have been scripted better by the best screenwriter in Hollywood.

Ivan had helped build his childhood house, but by the time of the evacuation, he'd moved out to Pripyat. So he didn't know what exactly his family had left behind or what artifacts he'd find. He began to solve the mystery as soon as we walked into the house, passing a front porch and kitchen still decorated and filled with expired food and rusty kitchenware. Ivan ignored this for the moment and beelined to his old bedroom, dimly lit by a single shaft of golden light streaming through the window.

On a table next to the window were piles of his old books, papers and photos covered in dust. On the corner of the table sat a perfectly preserved black and white picture of himself as a child, perhaps waiting for him to return, all these years later.

Olena stood carefully and quietly behind her husband, acknowledging that he deserved to experience this moment privately, despite all of us surrounding him. For a brief moment, I understood the power of marriage, how two people can find and empower each other, living both individually and as one. This couple had been through so much: they'd raised a child and built a home in the fallout of a nuclear disaster and failed state. Watching Ivan slowly move through the room, Olena slowly wiped away her own tears before wiping radioactive dust off the ancient photos of her husband.

Despite how built up this moment was, seeing Ivan in his old home, I'm not sure any of us were really ready for it. It was like stepping into the freeze-frame of a different world.

Ivan and Olena weren't able to keep any mementos from this house—I'm not sure if it's a law or just common sense—but the portraits I captured of them together, standing in diffused light near an old window, seemed enough for them. They knew they would probably never return. This part of their lives was behind them.

After packing a few memory cards, we drove off to our next destination in Pripyat, where we'd meet up with their son, Anton. Anton works at the power plant and is a close friend of Lucas's. He wasn't able to join us to visit his father's home, but he wanted to tag along to Pripyat.

We first headed to Ivan's apartment. In the city, it was a little easier to find our way. Although some streets were still navigable, nature was slowly taking back most things. Trees were emerging in the middle of walkways, and weeds overtook any crack they could fill.

Once we found Ivan's old apartment building, we followed him up the dilapidated stairway and into his former unit. Without skipping a beat, he calmly and naturally went into every room to close the windows, as if to protect the place from a storm. We spent about 45 minutes listening to Ivan tell us about his life in the city, his neighbors and how it felt to be back after all this time. I enjoyed photographing him and his son together here, in what was otherwise a stark, empty place.

Next, we were off to find Olena's apartment, which took a little more time to find. In true Soviet fashion, many of the buildings looked the same. As we encountered the outside of her building, she pointed out that the chair sitting outside the front was hers, and that some looter must have once tried to take it away.

Olena's apartment looked a little less decayed than Ivan's, with some walls still painted in a lively bright blue, and rooms where the wallpaper still struggled to hang on. Olena cried as she slowly walked across every inch of her old flat. She and Ivan pointed out spots where they remembered sitting and drinking coffee together as a young couple, and how they were separated for nearly six months after the evacuation before being reunited.

I shot a few portraits of Anton and his mother in the fashion I did with his dad. Their mere presence in this building, so rich with personal and global history, was an astonishing feat, and elevated my simple photographs into documents that are now connected to an impressive history that's quickly fading into the past.

ON AN AFTERNOON VISIT to the nearby city of Chernobyl, after which the plant was named, we visited many haunting memorials. The most striking was the Wormwood Star Memorial complex. A dirt road runs through the central section, flanked by signs commemorating the nearly 200 villages evacuated because of radiation fallout. One side of each sign is white, representing life in the village before the accident, and the other side is black with a red line crossing through the name of the village, symbolizing the emptiness afterward.

From the west, the Trumpeting Angel monument stands tall and proud, with a few more monuments surrounding the site, among them a famous sculpture called Tamer of a Bull.

In the middle of the complex is the postal area, filled with empty mailboxes into which you can throw a letter to the defunct addresses of liquidated settlements. Befitting the theme of lost ages, the last standing statue of Vladimir Lenin in Ukraine is also in the city of Chernobyl.

The streets are nearly empty, but there are still a few people who live here.

Workers inside this part of the zone follow a strict routine—15 days in the city, 15 days out of the zone. Everyone is tested for radiation as they leave.

The days were flying by, but few of them involved the power plant itself. The closest I got was on the train each morning, catching a quick glimpse of the plant through the passing trees. But eventually, finally, the day came that would change all that: we'd be visiting the inside of the structure that had loomed over the horizon our entire trip.

On April 25, 1986, reactor 4 was to be shut down for routine maintenance. Officials decided to use the opportunity to test whether it could provide enough power to operate the reactor core cooling system during a transition between a loss of main station electrical power supply and starting up the emergency power supply provided by diesel engines.

Unfortunately, there was a miscommunication between the personnel in charge of the test and the people in charge of the reactor. The operators ended up deviating from established procedures, while a lack of safety protocols meant a sudden and uncontrollable surge swept across the reactor, causing a swift explosion and near-total destruction of the reactor. The error was compounded by the materials involved in the reactor, such as graphite, which landed throughout the area, seeping radioactive materials into the environment.

To visit this ossified building, we had to pass through many levels of security and carefully change out from our civilian clothes (in a series of different rooms) into double-layered protective uniforms, special boots with plastic covers, thick gloves, hard hats and breathing masks. I assumed we were using the best possible protection available, since we were being given extremely rare access to parts of the plant that very few visitors get to explore.

Our guide throughout the plant was a man named Stanislav "Stavi" Shekstello, a close friend of Lucas's and the public relations manager for the Chernobyl plant. Back in November 2016, Stavi and Lucas were riding the train together and had a pivotal conversation. Stavi was explaining how a coworker of his, Tatyana, who worked in the plant during the 1980s, now needed $1,000 for a life-saving thyroid operation. Living on a meager $50 a month, she turned to her community for help. Lucas was so moved by the story that he helped raise enough money for her surgery. That same year, the Clean Futures Fund was born.

In person, Stavi beamed with tremendous pride, knowledge and openness. He was the perfect guide for what often felt like an ominous tour. Entering the older parts of the plant felt like we were stepping back in time into a cutting-edge crown jewel of Soviet nuclear power.

Joining the four reactors is the main thoroughfare, hundreds of meters long, known as the "golden corridor," walled with endless slabs of golden aluminum. Walking slowly down that hallway in our protective gear, our footsteps echoed heavily throughout the decrepit sheen. I remember every footstep. The weight of the moment felt as strong as being in downtown New York on 9/11—the inescapable feeling that I was connected to something historic. Next to that tragic day in 2001, this tour of Chernobyl may have been the most consequential day of my life.

We first entered control room 3. The room resembled what a shlock movie director from the 1970s would think a scientific control room looked like: dull fluorescent lights, broad gray tables, oversized knobs and chunky red switches, all of which seemed incomprehensible to the average person. For the most part, all this machinery, from the monitors to the telephones, remained intact and, theoretically, still functional. Ukraine relied heavily on the plant for nationwide electricity even after the explosion, and so the three remaining reactor units, apart from the ill-fated number 4, continued to operate for an oddly long time: number 2 shut down in 1991, number 1 in 1996 and number 3 in 2000.

It was then time to continue down to control room 4, which was surprisingly close. We passed through additional levels of security, as guards checked our paperwork and the credentials on our trusty *programa*. We also needed to step back and forth on wet and dry towels laid down on the floor whenever we entered or exited these parts of the plant, to reduce the chance of spreading any contamination.

Control room 4 astonished me. It seemed unbelievable that I was really there. Back in control room 3, Lucas and Stavi were able to explain the design, the panels, how all the different controls functioned. But here, everyone fell silent. Jeff, Rita and I respectfully documented the emptiness of the room, while Stavi stood curiously still in the middle and Lucas took measurements with his Geiger counter. (The readings were significantly higher there than anywhere else we'd visited.) There was an undeniably haunting feeling emanating from every corner.

As we prepared to exit the room, Lucas stopped us. "I just want you to experience this," he said quietly. "Like, no cameras—just feel this. Because it's easy to get caught up in taking the photos, but I want you to feel this. I want you to imagine the explosion, the shaking, the lights, the ceiling falling. I want you to imagine people running from station to station. I want you to imagine the shift supervisor, standing right behind where Jeff is standing. I want you to imagine they don't know what to do. I want you to imagine they don't exactly know what's going on. So they go to their training. They do what they think they're supposed to do. You've got guys running the turbines; you've got guys running the control assemblies. There would've been that mechanical background, the ambient noise. There would've been rumblings. There would've been shaking. And there would've been confusion. So just for a second, I just want you to feel that. 'Cause otherwise this is just another room."

One of our last stops was to the unfinished water-cooling towers that were under construction at the time of the accident. They were enormous. Much like the vacant ghost towns that have transformed into ecological specimens, this half-finished project has today morphed into something beautiful. As I gazed up through my camera lens, I snapped a photo from inside the tower, peering up at a darkened halo surrounding a beautiful blue sky with white puffy clouds. Below that, a graffiti artist painted a makeshift monument on the dirty concrete and exposed rebar: the face of a first responder, determined and optimistic.

THE NEXT DAY, WE WERE SET to travel forward in time and visit the New Safe Confinement—the Arch, as it's called, because it resembles a giant airplane hangar. More than 40 governments pitched in $1.6 billion to build the 350-foot-tall, 850-foot-wide structure, which took more than 10,000 workers to construct. Its lifespan, boosted by a dizzying array of complex materials, is projected at 100 years at least. Ukrainian President Petro Poroshenko called it "the biggest moving construction that humanity has ever created."

The Arch encompasses not just the remains of reactor 4, but also the aging shelter that the government hastily built in the immediate aftermath of the accident. To be built around the old, aging structure, the New Safe Confinement had to be large enough to cover everything and then some—engineers had to add extra height to accommodate cranes that would later deconstruct the old tomb within this new one.

The Arch began construction in 2010 and took the better part of a decade to complete. In fact, during my visit, it wasn't even finished. (They completed the project in July 2019. In hindsight, seeing how COVID-19 would shut down construction projects worldwide less than a year later, they didn't finish a moment too soon.)

During our tour of the area in the morning, I quickly noticed striking differences about this construction site from what we'd seen earlier, from the modern equipment right down to the uniforms of the workers. It was evident how the whole world had come together, financially and spiritually, to help create something ultra-modern to help contain the site. Nuclear fallout, after all, knows no borders.

Once inside the Arch, we had to pass through several rooms, like layers of protection against what awaited inside. When we crossed the final checkpoint and radiation detectors, we finally made our way inside the center portion of the Arch, where I was standing face-to-face with the ominous yet strangely familiar original shelter—colloquially dubbed the sarcophagus.

The sarcophagus is a giant metal and concrete structure that was built under hazardous conditions, with very high levels of radiation and severe time constraints. Its design began on May 20, 1986, just three weeks after the disaster. It is estimated that within the shelter there are tons of radioactive corium, contaminated dust and exposed uranium and plutonium. But before construction could even begin, they needed to build a cooling slab under the reactor to prevent the hot nuclear fuel from burning through the foundations. Four hundred coal miners were called upon to dig the required tunnel below the reactor, and by June 24, the necessary 168-meter-long tunnel was in place. By November 1986, the structure was complete. But two years later, Soviet scientists publicly recognized its flaws, revealing the structure would need to be replaced in as little as two decades.

While snapping a few photos of the sarcophagus, all I could think about were the liquidators who risked their lives here over the years. "Liquidators" is the term given to the hundreds of thousands of Soviet soldiers and civilians, most of them drafted, who cleaned up the site. The liquidators are widely credited with limiting both the immediate and long-term damage from the disaster. After finishing their duties, they qualify for significant social benefits, like super-veterans. Indeed, many liquidators were praised as heroes by the Soviet government and the press—yet many others have struggled for years to have their participation officially recognized. One of the main projects that the Clean Futures Fund is involved in is helping provide direct support and resources for the liquidators now living in Slavutych.

Our time in the Arch was short—just 15 minutes, due to the risk of exposure. The whole scene was dark and a little hectic. After a quick glimpse inside the ground zero of nuclear disasters, we were shuffled out, and made our way back to Slavutych.

UNLIKE THE CITY OF Chernobyl, whose rich history dates back to the 12th century, Slavutych did not even exist before 1986. It was purpose-built after the nuclear disaster to house survivors and evacuees from Pripyat. This remains true in 2020—of everyone who evacuated, about 8,000 were children, many of whom still live in Slavutych today.

Consequently, and unsurprisingly, residents of Slavutych suffer from above-average levels of radiation-related illnesses. In some ways, they are trapped by their circumstances; many inhabitants still work at the site of the former plant for monitoring, maintenance or scientific purposes.

But the city, at least, is not dreary. From its beginnings in the 1980s, Slavutych was designed as a mea culpa from the Soviet government, which spared no expense to construct an ultra-modern city from scratch. Residents enjoyed modernist architecture, front lawns, playgrounds and sports facilities—unheard of elsewhere in the country. Today, they also have an annual film and urbanism festival and local soccer club, FC Slavutych.

It is also, of course, home base for the Clean Futures Fund.

Among the CFF's many goals is helping to improve the lives of locals in its own city. They fund a rehabilitation center for children and young adults, which, during my visit, was being run by a warm and gracious woman named Anna Dmitrievna, whom I could immediately tell was perfect for her job.

Beyond the communal spaces, we were warmly welcomed into the homes of several survivors and children that the Clean Futures Fund is helping. One notable young man was named Andre. Nearly every day we were in Ukraine, Lucas would get a phone call or voicemail from Andre. Lucas talked about Andre often and explained some of his disabilities to us, which included the ability to walk. Andre underwent several procedures before our visit, and we all hoped that his leg braces would be delivered during our time there. Unfortunately, they were not, but we did get to visit Andre and his mother at their house and witness the bond between Lucas and this family firsthand.

We accompanied Lucas and others from the CFF on a few home visits like this, knocking on doors and stepping into private worlds filled with hope, nobility, and trauma. The CFF helps many older power plant workers raise funds for operations and medications, and it facilitates connections when possible. They have a medical director, Dr. Viktoria Beznoshchenko, who was herself one of the leading physicians from the nuclear plant. She accompanies the CFF staff into many of these homes to help when she can.

We were warmly welcomed at every door, and I was fascinated by the diversity of their homes: some were decorated in a colorful and rustic traditional Ukrainian style, while others (mostly belonging to younger locals) were modern European dwellings. These are the generations of Chernobyl.

We got a taste of the old style of living on a brisk Sunday morning, when we were invited to attend services at a new church in the city. It turned out to be one of my favorite things to photograph during the entire project. It was designed in a dynamic Russian Orthodox style, adorned with glistening gold domes and an ultra-modern, almost minimalist facade. I'd seen a few churches on this trip already, but I was not prepared for the splendor of what was inside this one. It was possibly the most amazing church I'd ever seen: a massive chandelier hung between crisp white composite columns, while carved-out engravings across smaller columns lining the walls drew the eye in every direction. Wondrous light streamed in through the windows, illuminating some of the paintings and icons, which depicted Jesus helping the sick children and first responders of Chernobyl as the infamous explosion is visible in the background. This hyper-localized interpretation of Christianity drove home the severity of the accident, its lasting generational trauma and the overwhelming power of faith.

It makes sense that so many locals would continue to believe in religion, instead of turning away in anger or frustration. Several attendees of that church—really, many of the residents of Slavutych—continue to work near the plant as liquidators, cleaning up radioactive residue and debris. It's not a job you could perform stoically. You need to believe in a higher cause, that you're truly doing good work and helping others, even if you know you're sacrificing your own health. In that sense, it is a profoundly Christian career.

We met with several liquidators during our time in the city. They hold meetings where they can voice their frustrations and offer each other support, and we attended a few to get a sense of their concerns. Community is vital here: retired liquidators' monthly pensions are not high enough for them to survive, especially for anyone with serious health issues. The CFF steps in when they can—we saw Lucas and his staff donate some money to the neediest liquidators, whose portraits I captured afterwards. But donations are not consistent, and life is hard.

Most liquidators describe the accident and years afterward as "the war"—unfortunately, they were fighting an invisible enemy. In most cases, it took years, even decades for these selfless fighters to realize exactly how much damage the radioactive enemy had inflicted upon them.

It's hard to quantify all this, which makes activism that much trickier. After the fall of the USSR, it became difficult to evaluate the status of liquidators' health—mostly because they are not citizens of Russia, whose government has always been notoriously vague about the disaster. Hard statistics have become scarce. According to Vyacheslav Grishin, the leader of the union of Chernobyl liquidators in Russia, about 60,000 are dead, and some 165,000 are disabled. But the true effects are almost certainly greater, and we may never fully understand the complete picture.

WRITING THIS IN 2020, it's clear that the lessons learned from Chernobyl were not taken to heart by governments around the world. The parallels between COVID-19 and Chernobyl are clear: a communist government keeps a lethal outbreak secret, to the detriment of not just its own citizens but the entire world. The threat is lethal, invisible, airborne and contagious. Lockdowns and quarantines are needed to restrict the spread. Plastic barriers are taped up around hospitals. People start wearing masks, afraid of air itself. First responders, like in 9/11, risk their lives to save others.

Some have called the coronavirus "China's Chernobyl moment." But during my visit, in 2018, none of this was even thinkable. I was focused on the past and present, not the future. And to tie my whole story together, I searched for something, or someone, who could help bring my story full circle.

My answer was a woman named Adele.

Adele was one of the liquidators from the community meeting. One afternoon, we drove over to her modest flat on the outskirts of town. Dressed in a bright pink striped sweater, she greeted Jeff, Rita and I with a huge smile. As soon as I walked inside, I noticed many similar sweaters hanging around, as if decorating the space. Before I realized what was happening, Adele sprung up with a tailor's tape measure, taking our sizes and trying to match us with what I learned were her handmade sweaters.

It was an enchanting gesture, but we were there on business. So once Jeff and I set up our cameras and I found the best light in the room, we asked if we could start filming and photographing her. She replied, in perfect English (but with a heavy Ukrainian accent), "No. First we have conversation." So, of course, we respected her wishes, spending the next two hours sipping coffee, talking, laughing and listening to her stories. She had worked at the Chernobyl plant for many years, before, during and after "the war." She had buried a son. She had a grandson with disabilities that needed help. A close relative was infected with HIV and could not access the necessary medications.

She had many health issues herself, and was embarrassed of

her teeth, although she loved to laugh. Like many others, she could barely survive on her monthly pension. But she found hope where she could: she taught herself to knit those beautiful wool sweaters, which she would never sell—only give away. She spent three months in Texas in the U.S. with a host family, which is how she learned English. She reflected warmly on her childhood summers spent in Odessa, a port city in Southern Ukraine, famous for its beaches.

Beneath the veneer of happiness, I could tell that the loss of Adele's son seemed to permanently scar her in some way. In that way, she reminded me deeply of my own mother. When I was just one year old, my older brother was killed while riding his bicycle, and my mom never fully recovered. For her remaining years, she too was traumatized by this needless tragedy. Perhaps Adele and my mother, if they ever met, would have had a lot to talk about. Or perhaps they wouldn't have talked at all—but merely by looking at each other, they would know each other's pain, and that would bring a small comfort to them both.

We learned all of this and much more about Adele that day. She was eager to share her story with us, to ensure her life meant something, had meaning beyond its tragic pitfalls. For me, she was brave. She was Ukraine. She was Slavutych. She was the Clean Futures Fund. She was Chernobyl. She was resilient.

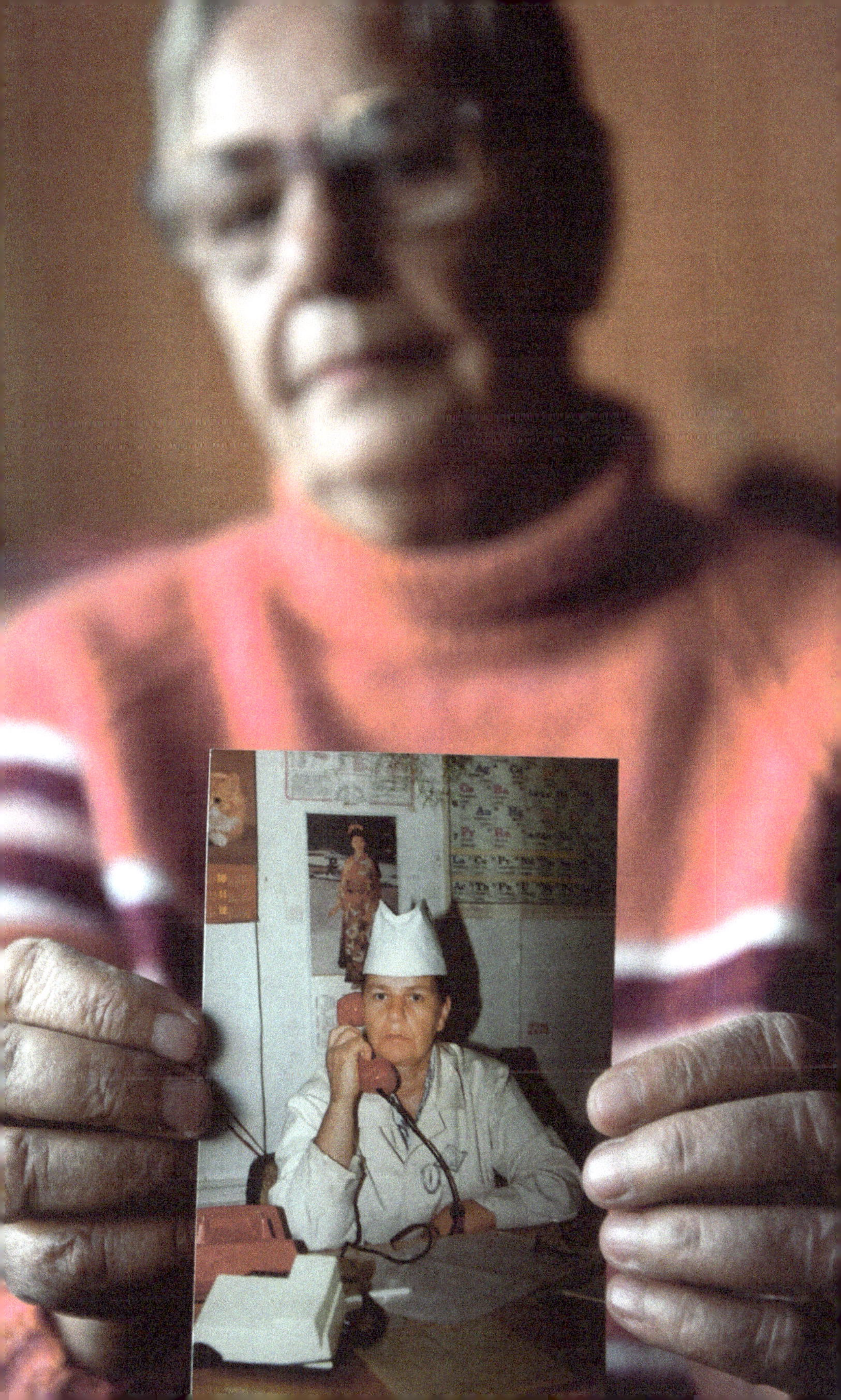

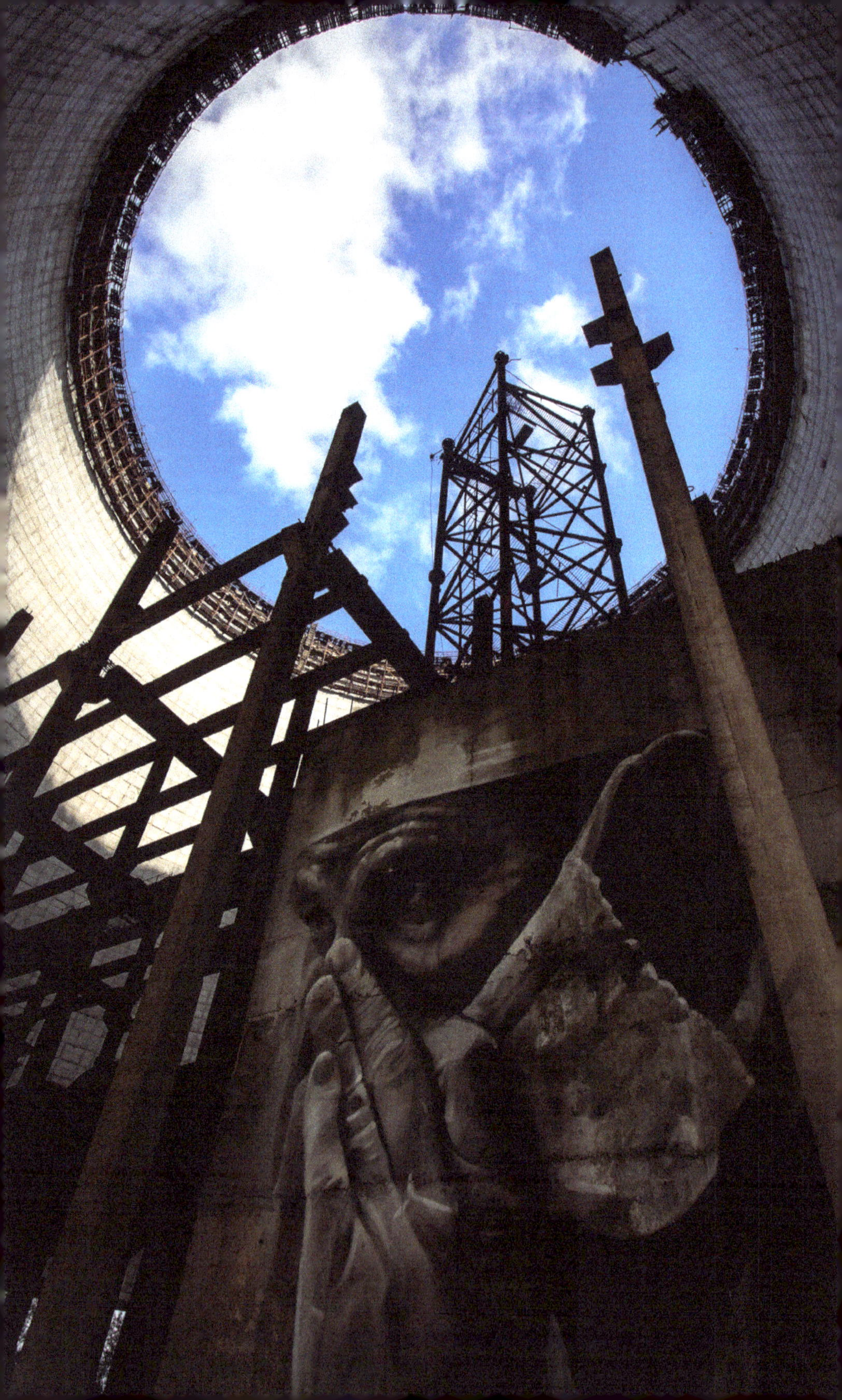

PHOTO TIP: PHOTOJOURNALISM

One of my most affecting assignments as a photojournalist was to Srebrenica, the small Bosnian town where 8,000 people were massacred in 1995. Srebrenica is Bosnia's Auschwitz, ground zero for a horrific genocide that continues to scar the Balkan nation. I visited in 1996, mere months after the war had ended. Officials had just discovered its now-infamous mass grave, and my job was to photograph it. I couldn't believe what I was seeing: I watched international aid workers and locals excavate this blood-soaked dirt, and it scarred me in a way I wouldn't feel again until 9/11.

I visited Sarajevo, too, where the longest siege in modern warfare resulted in the deaths of 10,000 people. The city's Olympic stadium, used to welcome athletes from all around the world less than a decade earlier, was now a makeshift graveyard. Families wailed as their loved ones were buried underneath way-finding signs for the bygone Olympic games. I was instructed to wear a bulletproof vest during my visit, as a few holdout snipers still lurked in the mountains surrounding the city. At night I stayed at the Jewish Community Center in Sarajevo, sleeping on the floor. It didn't have running water or a working bathroom.

In this book, I don't talk too much about my photojournalism years—partly because they were so long ago, and also because I want to focus on optimism and resilience. But they were formative years for me, and taught me valuable lessons about photography, travel and the way the world works. It also opened my eyes and heart to the world of geopolitics, and the wonderful photographers who are fighting to document these stories that might otherwise go unnoticed.

One place I get to indulge in all this is the Xposure International Photography Festival, held annually in the United Arab Emirates. I was recently invited to speak about my Chernobyl project alongside Jeff, the documentary filmmaker. The Xposure curator found Jeff's work on Instagram; one thing led to another, and soon he and I were hugging again in the UAE after not seeing each other for a year.

Our talk went seamlessly, despite my fear of public speaking, and I loved watching all the other remarkable presentations. I was lucky to meet Michael Christopher Brown, whose inspiring work from Cuba and Libya's 2011 civil war I felt most connected to; and wildlife photographer Ami Vitale, whose work on pandas and the fragile state of Sri Lankan peace has earned her multiple World Press Photo awards.

While there, I pitched my series on 9/11 to the curator for the

2021 Xposure festival, to mark the 20th anniversary of that fateful day. He told me they often don't invite the same photographers back, but he liked my idea—so he made an exception, and I'll be heading back next year, assuming the pandemic cools down. I truly hope it does, so I'll be able to meet and speak on the same stage as the legendary Steve McCurry, who shot the infamous "Afghan Girl" that graced the cover of *National Geographic*, and veteran war photojournalist James Nachtwey, who's won the World Press Photo of the Year award numerous times.

I'm humbled by these industry titans, and the global impact of their work far outweighs my own. But for me, these professionals are also inspirational. They show us what humans are capable of, and their work is a testament to the power of photography and the importance of empathy. Genocide among foreign tribes half a world away is regrettably easy to ignore—until you see it for yourself.

SO DESPITE THIS BOOK not being too much about photojournalism, I'd like to touch on the subject and offer some advice and insight for those curious about the profession.

The keyword of photojournalism is *access*. Access is everything. I write the word "access" all over my to-do lists and journals—anywhere I can. If I meet someone with access to a story I'm interested in, I need to get to know them better. I don't believe anything in life is a coincidence. People are put into our lives for a reason. In my case, that reason is for me to tell their stories.

Access will redefine your story. It's the difference between snapping some holiday mementos on a trip to Cuba and meeting a local who invites you into her house. It means hearing firsthand accounts of the Chernobyl disaster from people who were there; spending hours riding from one rural town to another with NGO staffers who live there; meeting a woman on a plane who invites you to watch a school being built in India. That's access. In a word, it's trust.

In order to earn that trust, you have to put yourself out there. You have to be comfortable approaching strangers and being told no. You have to hunt around and strike up conversations with anyone who looks interesting. If you're shy, you'll have to learn to break out of your shell—at least when you're out shooting. If the meek will indeed inherit the earth, the earth probably won't have many photojournalists.

If all this sounds a little relentless—well, it can be. But that's because photojournalism can be relentless. You have to keep working, keep practicing your art. The more you photograph, the better you will be. You have to shoot and think differently. You have to challenge yourself in every shoot. Remember: you are only as good as your last photograph.

Some people see the camera as a barrier, something in front of your face that blocks you from being in the moment. I understand what they mean, but it's more about balance. I see the camera as an introduction, a way to connect with people. I find people often open up to me when I want to take their photo—especially if I share it with them afterwards. That said, the most important moments of personal connection often happen when the camera is down and I'm not shooting.

To be a great photojournalist, in addition to access and practice, you have to know how to tell a story succinctly. The most powerful photojournalism pieces of recent years have told a massive story in a simple frame. Consider the infamous "Falling Man" taken on 9/11, of a man plunging headfirst down the side of one of the crumbling Twin Towers. Or the photo of Alan Kurdi, the three-year-old Syrian boy who drowned in 2015, at the height of Europe's refugee crisis. The tragic image of this young boy's corpse, lying on its stomach on the beach, made front pages worldwide. Both these images are incredibly sad, but they conveyed entire stories within them.

Not all great photojournalism is depressing, of course. If you're a basketball fan, think about the 2019 NBA Eastern Conference Semifinals, when Kawhi Leonard made "the shot" at the buzzer on Game 7. The faces of everyone in that frame—hope, frustration, astonishment, tension—tells the story of one of the most intense seconds of basketball history.

What these photos do is the same thing every great journalistic photo should do: take the viewer on a journey. They transport the audience to the time and place that particular image was taken.

When you're composing a shot, look through the viewfinder and decide what you want to include. What elements of the subject are necessary? If it's not important to your message, try to get it out of your frame. (This means moving around street lamps and garbage cans, or pivoting to exclude people who aren't part of the story.) If you can't control the scene—for instance, if you're covering a protest—then everything becomes part of your story.

Photojournalism and candid photography (or street photography) are very different beasts than portraiture and landscape photography. You need to move quickly. Your instincts have to be sharp. You may want to shoot on shutter priority mode, to ensure everything you shoot is in focus.

I greatly enjoyed my years as a photojournalist, but it's a hard life to keep up for very long. Not only is it physically demanding, but the job opportunities are scarce and I found it difficult to connect with people. It was more about the story and less about humanity. I much prefer longer-form photojournalism, like what I do with Photographers Without Borders, where I'm embedded somewhere for two weeks. Getting to know people and telling their stories is still photojournalism, but it's different than the daily grind. For me, it's more enjoyable.

I sincerely believe that photography has the power to

change the world. Photographers tell stories, document history and influence people to be more engaged with global events. The difference between the 20th century and today is that nobody waits for a weekly magazine to hit newsstands to learn about the world; everything is on Instagram and Twitter. I find this incredibly exciting: so many people are now budding photographers, armed with smartphones and an eagerness to share their experiences with the world. We are all storytellers. We are all photographers. And because of that, we all have the power to change the world.

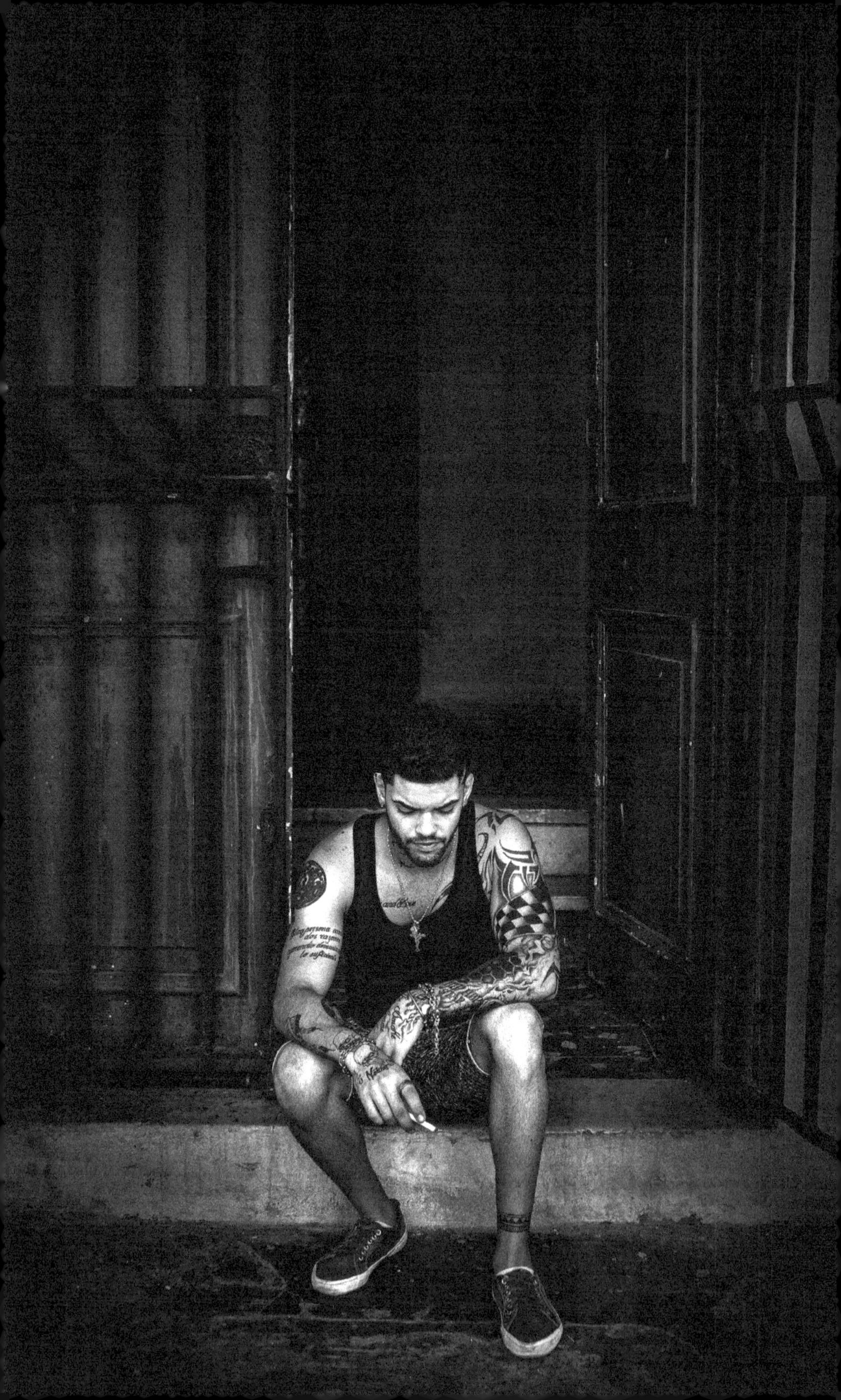

CHAPTER 9

NOSTALGIA IN CUBA

"Let the world change you and you can change the world."

– Ernesto Che Guevara

Havana, more than perhaps any city in the world, is in a remarkable transition. It is filled with incredible beauty, a little sadness and immense possibilities.

Unfortunately, because of political and historic circumstances, relatively few Americans have visited the country. There weren't direct flights a decade ago. In 2010, just 60,000 Americans visited, necessarily by detouring through Canada or Mexico. But in the last few years, after President Barack Obama began to thaw relations between the two countries in 2014, that number has multiplied tenfold. Even despite Donald Trump's attempts to once again cut ties with the island nation, more than 600,000 Americans visited in both 2017 and 2018. I think that's great for both countries: thousands of Cubans are now meeting Americans for the first time, and understanding that really, on a personal level, there is so much more that unites us than what separates us. Americans, meanwhile, can finally speak with the people who've been living just 90 miles off the coast of Florida, and realize they aren't Cold War–era communist villains after all. They're just people. Beautiful, warm, friendly people.

I wish I could have visited sooner. Having grown up so close, and still spending so much of my time in Florida today, Cuba feels like a neighbor I just didn't bother getting to know. Now I'm sorry I didn't take the time to better understand them.

If you haven't visited, just imagine this: endless color, crumbling relics, and infectious smiles. The scent of gasoline swirls with tobacco fumes and a hint of cheap perfume. The sound of bongos overlaps with passionate conversation. It's all here, and it makes you wonder: how does it work? The answer is unknowable. It just does.

You can see the passion of the place in an elderly person's wrinkled face, in a young adult's tattoos, in every child's eyes. This is Cuban life. They just make it work. They have no choice. They are scrappy, independent, full of tremendous soul and strength. Their innovative spirit is what keeps 70-year-old cars running and 100-year-old homes standing. There are many lessons to be learned here, and I can tell you firsthand, the Cuban people are eagerly waiting for you to hear their stories.

Oportunidad oozes from every pore here. There are so many

reminders that Havana was once a world-class city—arguably on par with Paris or Rome—and I am certain it will be again. It won't happen quickly, but it will happen. The sense of knowledge, history and intelligence is evident in every landmark. Culture, creativity and imagination are evident on every street corner. Each year brings exponentially more construction, much-needed renovations and, in some cases, just a fresh coat of paint for now, as the people of this tropical (read: *very* hot in the summer) nation prepare for us to join them in conversation over a mojito or café con leche.

Almost everybody asked me, "*De donde eres?*" ("Where are you from?"), and when I said "*Estados Unidos*" a look of pure joy came over their faces. I heard, over and over again, "I love America"; "My brother lives in Cleveland"; "Welcome"; "Oh my God"; "My cousin is in Miami"; "The past is the past, we are family again." My personal favorite: "What do you think of Cuba?" That's when I could finally use the word "*fantastico.*" (I don't think I've ever used the English equivalent in casual conversation, but here it seems like the only option.)

I have traveled quite a bit in my days, but Cuba made me nostalgic, the way I felt when visiting Eastern Europe in the 1990s, seeing newly opened countries like Romania and Bulgaria, where most people weren't used to seeing a tall American with a camera walking around. To that end, I also felt it was necessary to better understand this country by researching and watching documentaries about it after I got home. You cannot visit Cuba independently and not become absorbed in its multifaceted history, rife with tales of the American mafia, Spanish colonials and communist revolutionaries. Not since I was in Bosnia in 1996 have I felt like it's my duty to try and understand a complex country. It's truly unbelievable that I live so close yet remain a world away.

But before you think it's all smiles and salsa, let me assure you: this trip, for me, was also heartbreaking and an awakening of sorts. Havana is a full-force assault to the senses. It may not be for everyone.

There were moments near Parque Central, and in the swanky hotels, where I got a sense of what Havana used to be like, how it thrived in the good old days. I still believe it's possible that its best days lie ahead, and these current hardships will add to that success story. But it's not there yet. There is noticeable poverty and many people live in unsafe buildings. Weak supply chains keep grocery store shelves half-stocked at all times. Freedom of speech, if you're critical of *la Revolución*, is basically non-existent. And if you, the tourist, only stay in the expensive, state-owned hotels—if you stick to the beach and don't venture off into the city—you'll be cordoned off in a pseudo-paradise, where much of your money gets funneled to the governing regime instead of the people themselves.

Yes, there are definitely problems in Cuba. But progress is equally undeniable. It's not my intention to talk only about sadness or suffering, because there are so many wonderful things about Cuba, and those are the things I want to remember.

Yes, young lovers stroll the famous Malecon, holding hands and kissing; yes, the streets of Old Havana are crumbling (but are also being rebuilt); yes, the people are beautiful; yes, the classic cars are everywhere; yes, people really say "*dale*" like Pitbull; and yes, the coffee is strong as hell.

Somehow, all the stereotypes are true. And yet, when you're there, they don't feel like stereotypes at all. They just feel like everyday life.

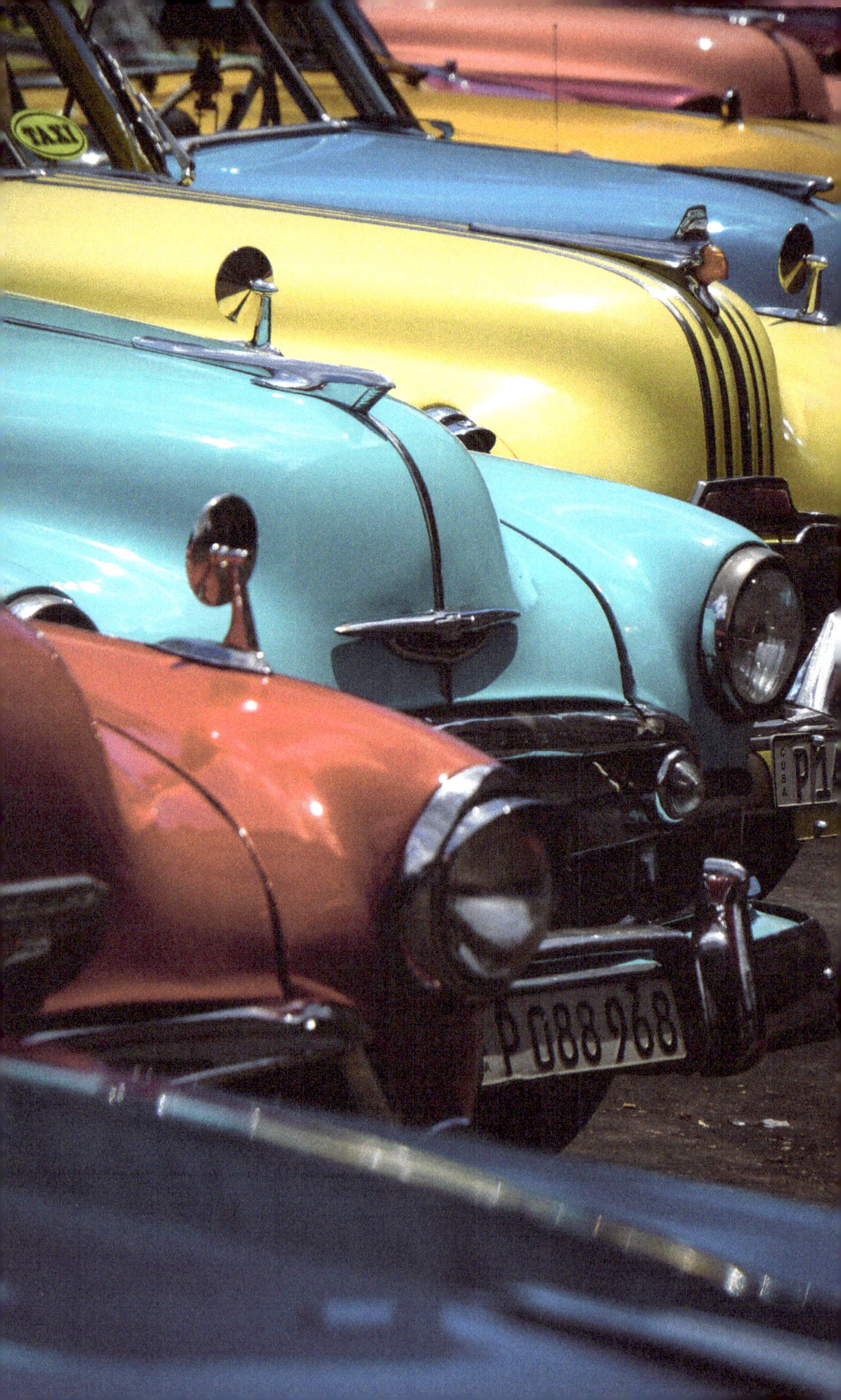
TAXI
P 088 968

PHOTO TIP: THE BYGONE BEAUTY OF MANUAL CONTROL

Cubans understand the value of working manually. Their beautifully kept-up classic cars often feature manual transmission, while even most rental cars for tourists are older, manual models. Public computers and WiFi are scarce. Technology is frozen in the 20th century, when society valued understanding the mechanics of a thing, its manual operations. Notwithstanding the fact that Cubans have no choice, they enjoy a great culture of understanding machinery well enough to fix it themselves, no matter what the problem may be.

Photographers could learn a thing or two from that. Like most modern photographers, I often rely on autofocus these days. But no matter how good your autofocus might be, you'll sometimes need to go manual.

Manual focus gives the photographer more control over the image, which can create an effect that might not otherwise work when the camera autofocuses. It can also be quicker to manually focus, especially if you have enough light to shoot at F/8 or higher, which will give you a greater depth of field. That depth of field might confuse the camera, but you can quickly hone in on exactly what you want in focus.

To focus manually, you first need to adjust your diopter to make sure everything you see through the lens is focused to your specific eyesight. (Anyone who needs glasses can attest to how nice it is to take them off when shooting accurately.) Next, make sure the auto/manual focus switch is set to "M" for manual, although some cameras have an "S," which stands for "single focus point," and a "C" for "continuous," which is useful for moving subjects.

Then, adjust the lens focus ring (remember, this is different from the zoom ring) until you get your subject in focus. It sometimes helps to move the ring a little beyond what looks right, so the subject blurs out of focus for a moment, to confirm that you're as close as possible to 100 percent tack-sharp focus.

When do I use manual focus? I choose the option if I know something or someone is going to be moving quickly, and I know where I want to frame subject—a finish line at the end of a race is a good example. When shooting weddings, I always photograph close-up images of the bride's jewelry and the couple's rings with my macro lens. I also manually focus these shots, because the depth of field in macro photography is very shallow (as low as F/1.2 or F/1.4), and it is critical that the plane of focus matches up with the subject.

Whether you choose manual or autofocus, these days we have

the luxury of checking our focus using LCDs and the zoom tool on the back of our DSLR or mirrorless cameras. It's a little safety net for everyone, but especially photographers who still appreciate the risks and rewards of manual focus.

IF YOU ENJOY SHOOTING with manual focus, you'll want to explore the shooting modes that give you more freedom and flexibility. It's always a shame to see someone buy a $2,000 camera and leave it on automatic—the beauty, and the fun, happens when you tinker with the manual options.

There are four common modes that give the artist some control: aperture priority ("A"), shutter priority ("S"), program ("P") and manual ("M"). I've used each one on all my cameras, but I typically stick with manual and aperture priority.

In program mode, the camera is going to do most of the work for you by selecting the aperture and shutter speed to achieve a proper exposure. There are still ways to tweak your exposure in program mode by rotating the command dial on the back of the camera right or left, and you can change the values if you decide you want a wider aperture or slower shutter. Overall, I find it still a little limiting when on assignments.

In shutter priority mode, you tell the camera what shutter speed you need—you might choose 1/2000 if you're at a sporting event—and the camera will select a corresponding aperture. Again,

I tend to stay away from this one, because I value being able to control the aperture of my images. I often want the lighting to be moodier, while the camera automatically strives to make everything as visible as possible.

In aperture priority mode, you can choose the aperture and control the depth of field you need. Remember, aperture is critical when shooting portraits or landscapes—both of which I love. For portraits, I prefer to shoot at F/4 or wider, to highlight the subject and blur the background. For large group shots or landscapes, my floor is F/8, to ensure the whole image is sharp. Just like shutter priority mode, in aperture priority, you select the aperture and the camera will provide a corresponding shutter speed to achieve a proper exposure.

One tool I've found very helpful in aperture priority mode is the exposure compensation, which allows you to either over- or under-expose the camera settings by three full stops, which comes in handy when the background is much brighter than the subject of your photograph.

Manual mode lets you control everything yourself: ISO, aperture, shutter speed and the rest.

When shooting manually, I choose my ISO first, depending on whether I am under a dust cloud on 9/11 or inside the containment arch of Chernobyl. If I spend the whole shoot in those same lighting conditions, I can set my ISO and forget about it. This is fairly common among photographers, and camera manufacturers know this, that is why the ISO adjustments are sometimes tucked away in a less convenient spot than the other two exposure settings.

Typically, I'll tend to choose the aperture next, to achieve the look I want. This will change pretty frequently, but if I'm shooting a series of portraits (like groomsmen getting ready), I'll have an idea of what look I want the whole set to have.

Finally, I adjust my shutter speed to match the lighting conditions available. I'm more flexible about this one, since my subjects tend to be either standing still or moving slowly. If my shutter speed is anywhere from 1/500 to 1/2000, it doesn't really make a difference. Shooting sports or wildlife, I'd have a different system.

I want to stress that these are just my own preferences, and there isn't always a clear-cut system for how this should work. Photography is an art. Art doesn't follow rules. If you want to shoot long exposures during the day, with buildings and people blurred out on a hectic street corner—go for it. If you want to make daytime look like night, that's your call. If you want to spend hours in post-production adding psychedelic colors to transform your daily shots into surreal dreamscapes, that's awesome.

Take these rules and break them, bend them, ignore them entirely. At the end of the day, photography should be about what you love—not what someone else tells you to do.

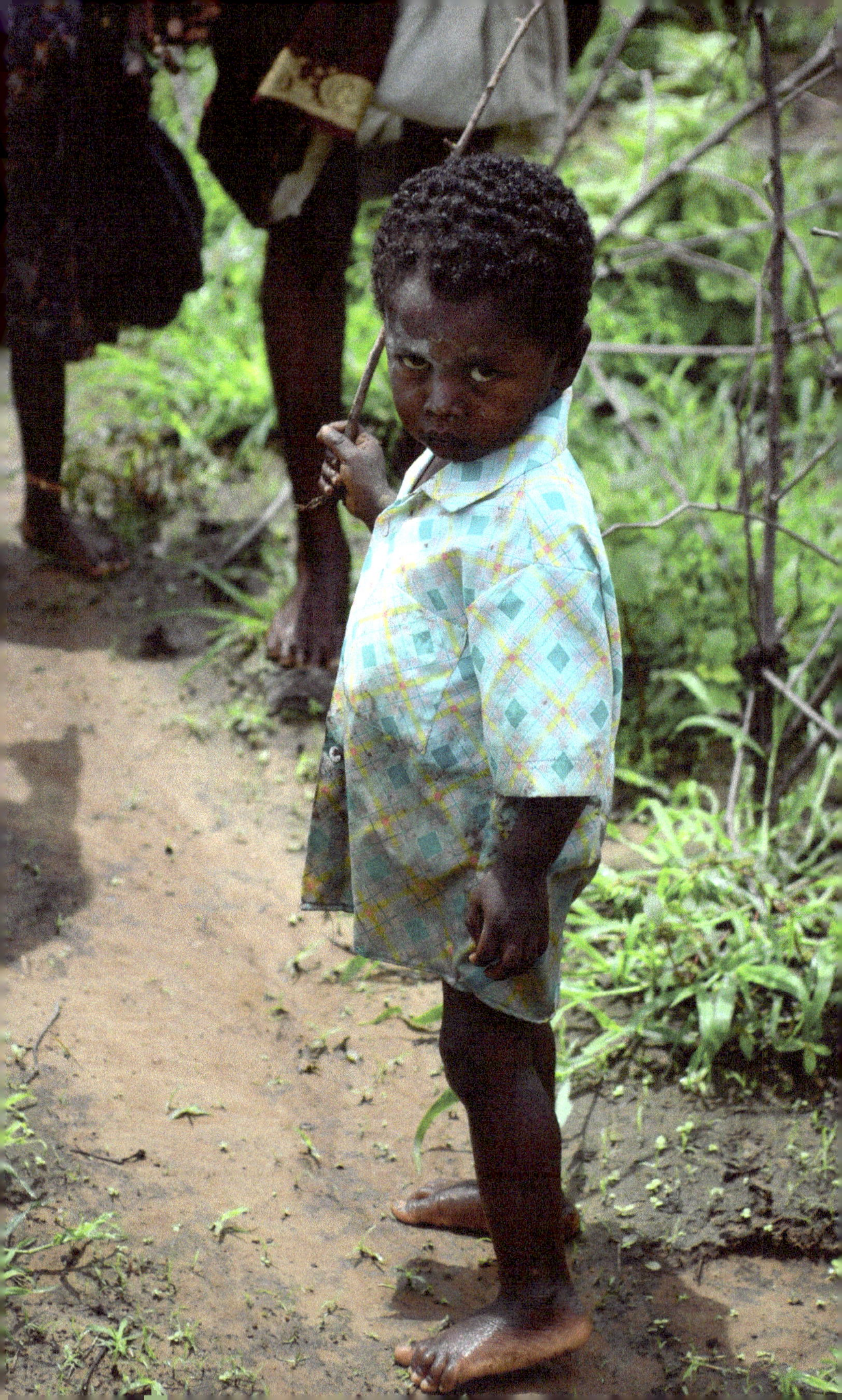

CHAPTER 10

MY FIRST TRIP TO INDIA

"Where there is love, there is life."
– Mahatma Gandhi

The culture shock in India is as real as everyone says. Every street is crowded; every road is bumpy; every driver honks their car horn as a courtesy, to let you know they're changing lanes or making a right turn or pissed off at you or thanking you. The distinct smells and sights are undeniable, whether you're in a big city or small town.

On my first trip to India, I enjoyed a little of both. Over a decade before my Photographers Without Borders assignment to the northern state of Bihar, I had a chance meeting with a woman named Tamara, who had established a small non-profit organization to help build schools in the country's south. She showed me a few photographs of the work they were doing. I was fascinated.

Months later, I arrived at the airport in the southern state of Goa and hopped into a car to settle in for the four-hour ride to the small community of Haliyal. Haliyal is a town of about 20,000 people in the southwestern state of Karnataka, and many of those residents can trace their roots to Africa. Descendants of slaves brought over by Portuguese merchants between the 16th and 19th centuries, they are today known as the Siddis of Karnataka. Their postcolonial circumstances situate them as mostly agricultural and menial workers, cementing their place in India's lowest caste tiers.

Schools are not always accessible, and the literacy rate in Haliyal is 66 percent—significantly lower than the state average of 75. Meanwhile, according to a survey of 800 public schools across 13 Indian states, key facilities such as washrooms and drinking water were not available in many schools or were in poor condition. Some had no playgrounds, others didn't even have toilets. Girls, in particular, would drop out at disproportionately higher rates than boys. On an even broader scale, when education isn't secure, children drop out early to enter the workforce, which can result in higher rates of child labor, homelessness and underage marriage.

I saw all this firsthand in Haliyal. They're not just statistics; it's reality. That's why Tamara's organization, Children's Poverty Relief, was building a new, modern school for a community plagued by aging, inadequate infrastructure. They wanted to build a brighter future for their children.

During my visit in 2007, construction crews were just starting the foundation. Men, women and children all pitched in to help move the building materials to the construction site, proudly carrying pails of sand and rocks, knowing their hard work would pay off the day the school doors swung open.

It was like no other construction site I'd seen. Kids gathered as if their favorite sport was watching these men and women toil around. Some of the youngest kids didn't even wear shoes, but as I watched their bare feet sink into the mud, I felt like the base of the structure would be forever strong. I also was struck by the colorful, well-worn clothing some children wore; a few agreed to pose for me behind a pile of sticks on a hill, as their mother looked on with hope—maybe this would be an optimistic "before" shot in a "before/after" series.

With the help of international volunteers and fundraising, people in the Global South can change the trajectory of their communities. They can break out of their castes, earn higher education and receive well-paying jobs to provide security in the future. I often wonder what their futures turned out to be—the children I met are probably teenagers now, could even be adults by the time I make it back to Haliyal one day. I'd love to see the progress they've made. Helping communities like these uplifts the entire planet. We take education for granted in the West, but it's important to remember that not everyone has the opportunities we have to learn and grow.

AFTER THAT TRIP TO HALIYAL, I got hooked on India. People tend to either love or hate the country—I definitely love it. I've visited several times, always eager to explore a different part of the subcontinent. But one of my favorite cities is its capital, New Delhi, where I traveled with Tamara after we finished our work in Haliyal.

Ancient and modern seamlessly merge in New Delhi, a symbol of India's rich past and flourishing present. It's been the nation's capital since 1931, when the colonial British rulers moved governance out of Calcutta, where political unrest led to political assassinations and instability.

Today it's a massive, sprawling metropolitan area of more than 26 million people (although the main city itself has fewer than 300,000). It's the biggest commercial city in India, with several large corporations headquartered there and endless shopping markets to browse. Add in some spicy street-side stalls, high-end restaurants and nonstop cultural festivals, and you have one of the world's great must-visit destinations.

Strolling the streets and parks, you will find happy kids whose joyous laughs make you want to be carefree again. Afternoons are always super-busy, as every square inch of the city is packed with commuters, shoppers and vendors. People will peek their heads out from apartment windows to wave at passersby. Beautiful women glide across sidewalks in a rainbow of Saris while shopkeepers call out their deals of the day. A visit to India will overwhelm your senses: aromas of cardamom, gasoline, chai, sweat and cinnamon waft through the air; car horns and hawking vendors shriek across the streets; the sidewalks are so overstuffed that one misstep can cause the whole line of dominos to tumble over. All of India is relentless and fascinating, and New Delhi is only more so.

To really dig deep into its history, a visit to Old Delhi is a must. The colorful bazaars, narrow lanes and old haveli mansions remind you of this city's rich history. You can learn more at the local historical museums and monuments: the India Gate, a memorial to those who died between the outbreak of the First World War and 1921; Parliament House, the impressive federal government headquarters; and Rashtrapati Bhavan, where the president lives, all offer glimpses into India's unique past and present.

We also stopped by Gandhi Smriti, the site where Mahatma Gandhi was assassinated in 1948. Gandhi lived in the house for several months before his death, and it took decades for the wealthy family that owned it to agree to sell it to the government. Ultimately, they made the right decision: today it's a free museum and prayer ground, surrounded by beautiful green grass and fruit trees.

Of course, no visit to Delhi would be complete with a trip to the Taj Mahal. The famous mausoleum, commissioned in 1632 by the Mughal emperor Shah Jahan to house his beloved wife's remains, is just a day trip from the city, about 150 miles south of Delhi in a city called Agra. It's more astounding in person than the photographs you've seen: the white marble seems to change color depending on the light and time of day, and every perspective makes for a wonderful snapshot. A UNESCO World Heritage Site, it is undeniably one of the world's most fascinating structures and a visible sign of India's distinguished history.

WHILE ON THAT SAME trip, I didn't want to leave the country without visiting the famous port city of Mumbai, formerly known as Bombay (the official name until 1995). The state capital of Maharashtra, Mumbai is a rambling, densely populated city on India's west coast and the capital of Bollywood—the "Bolly" actually comes from "Bombay."

The city—the most populous in India, with 18 million—is without question a destination to behold. On the waterfront of Mumbai Harbour stands the iconic Gateway of India stone arch, built by the British Raj in 1924. Offshore, the nearby Elephanta Island is home to ancient cave temples dedicated to Shiva. With ample modern bars and restaurants both high-end and traditional, the urban nightlife is just as exciting as its cultural landmarks.

I set out to photograph what I could from the moment I arrived. Children regularly ran toward me to have their pictures taken—one little boy who didn't want to be left out urged me to photograph him with his house visible in the background. In drizzling rain, an elderly man was not only happy to have his picture taken, but loved the shot and requested a copy of it.

I'm always happy to abide by these kindnesses. If I don't connect with my subjects, I may as well be spying on them. Photography, and all of art, is an opportunity to connect with strangers and create something beautiful together. There's an old travel expression: "Take only photographs, leave only footsteps." I like the sentiment, but I respectfully disagree. I'd rather take *and* leave photographs, offering something for these beautiful people to enjoy for years to come. After all, they've given me memories I'll cherish for a lifetime.

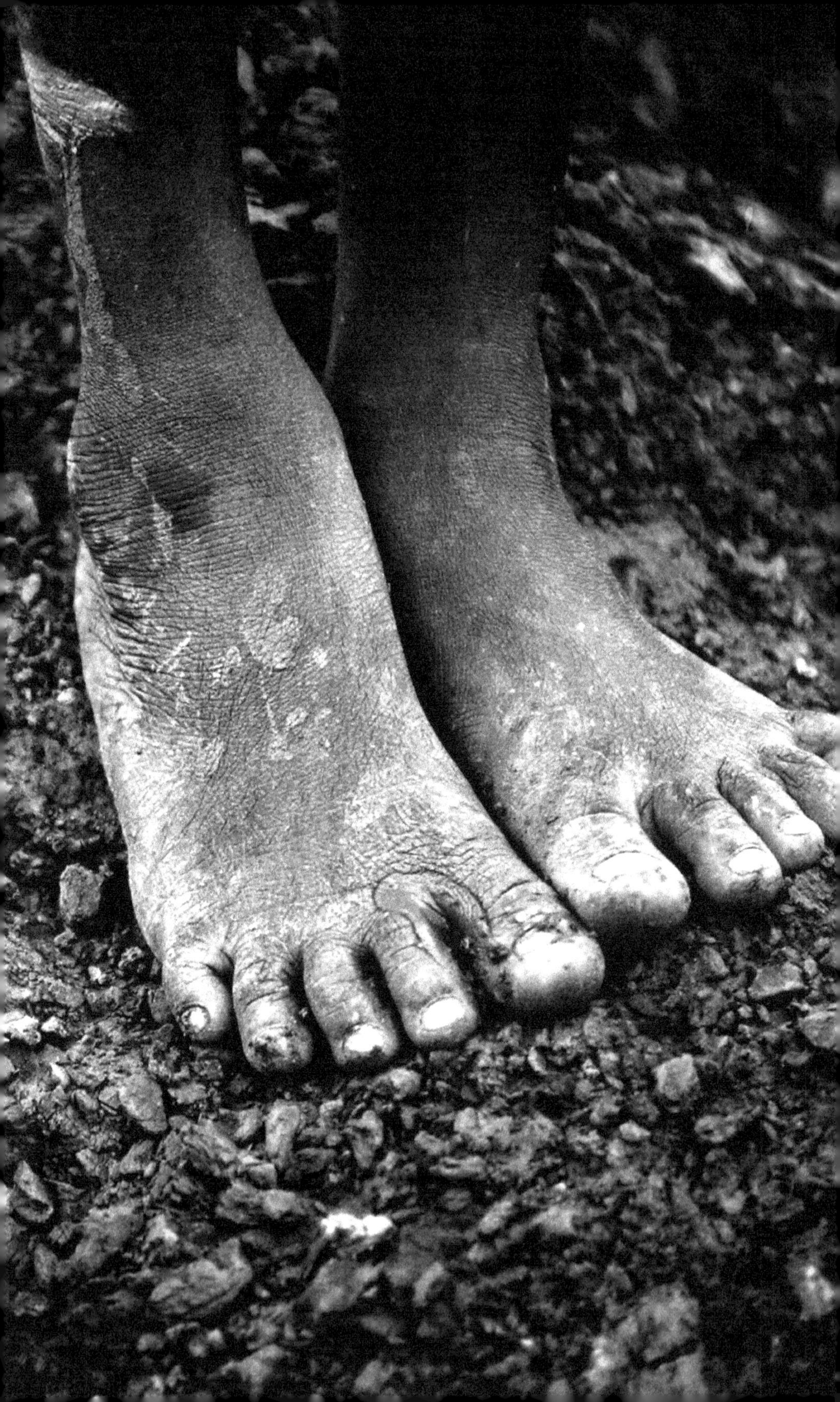

PHOTO TIP: FILM VERSUS DIGITAL

I began my career when film was the only choice. But even on that first trip to India in 2007, by which point I'd already transitioned to digital, I preferred to also shoot film using my Nikon F100. Some high-end photographers—such as expert wedding photographer Jose Villa, one of my mentors—are shooting film again and charging more money by billing themselves as fine-art wedding photographers. I appreciate the idea, though I'd rather keep my skill set broad: I'm confident about my work in color, black-and-white or chrome film in any camera.

If you're planning on shooting film, you'll first want to decide what film to use. There are several types of film and chrome (also known as slide film), and it can be confusing for those not familiar with the industry.

Even if you've decided on either traditional color or black-and-white film (or maybe C41 black and white, which can be developed at a color processing lab), you'll still have to decide on an ISO.

Each roll of film is marked with a number from 50 to 3200, which, like the ISO of digital cameras, indicates the film's speed and sensitivity to light. ISO 100 would be great in bright sunlight, because it is less sensitive to light. When I have an assignment to shoot film at a daytime event, such as a beach volleyball tournament at noon on a sunny day, I would choose a color film with an ISO of 100. Conversely, when I am shooting something indoors or on a very overcast day, I would prefer an 800-speed film, because I will need it to be more sensitive to trickier lighting conditions. With each number rating of the film, the sensitivity doubles, so a film with an ISO of 100 is twice as sensitive to light as a film with an ISO of 50, and so on.

My favorite high-speed film is a black-and-white film with an ISO of 3200, which I used a lot when capturing brides getting ready for their weddings. Film ISO functions the same way as digital ISO: the higher the number, the grainier the picture. But in black and white, this creates a beautiful, moody, human look that fits well with this situation. It also gives me the flexibility of shooting in darker spaces without a flash.

One trick I've often used when developing film is what's called "pushing" or "pulling" the film. For example, if you need an extra stop while shooting and you only have a roll of 400-speed film, you can lie to your camera and set it on 800. Essentially, you're telling your camera that the film inside it is more sensitive to light than it really is. This speeds up the exposures, exposing your film to less light. When you send your film to the lab, and you ask them to "push" it one stop, they will leave the film in the developer longer.

All this may sound a little dated today. But just like vinyl albums and sourdough bread, there seems to be a modern trend toward the analog systems of olden times. Film will never be as popular as it once was, but it still generates a beautiful, unique look that will remain sought after as long as photographers exist.

I STILL USE MY NIKON F100 film camera now and then, but I feel that digital cameras have surpassed film, especially in the 2010s. Sometimes I'll use a combination of hardware: I'll bring my SLR, DSLR, mirrorless, GoPro and even iPhone to tell a complete story. For my travels, I rely on my two Fuji mirrorless cameras, since they're lighter and the lenses are smaller—they allow me to walk around city streets and shoot without sticking out too much. (Well, any more than a tall white guy with a camera in India or Botswana normally would, anyway.) As technology advances, it's my opinion that mirrorless cameras will become the standard for professionals, displacing DSLRs.

SLR stands for "single lens reflex," and refers to the way old film cameras work. (The D in DSLR just stands for "digital," but the camera operates more or less identically.) Most classic SLRs are also known as a 35mm cameras because of the size of the film they take. When the shutter button is pressed, a mirror flips out of the way to reveal the film—or, in a DSLR, the sensor.

Shooting film still has some advantages. Specifically, I find it forces me to slow down and take my time to carefully get the exposure and composition right, because I've only got a limited number of film rolls and need to conserve each frame. In my experience, film photographers also enjoy a better personal life—without endless hours spent tweaking images in Photoshop, they can actually enjoy their free time. Just send the film off to get it developed and send the best results to the client.

To fully appreciate those positives, though, you also have to consider the digital alternative. Yes, having unlimited freedom to shoot thousands of images is arguably better for creativity and takes some mental pressure off every frame, but on the other hand, I feel like I become a worse shooter: I tend to fall into repetitive cycles, shooting variations of a shot without paying much attention to composition. I also resent how long it takes to back up all my media cards to hard drives before editing them all on a computer. Regrettably, I'd estimate that maybe 15 percent of my time these days is spent actually shooting, while the rest is spent sitting at the computer.

Yes, I know some people love Photoshop. There are even whole waves of digital artists for whom photography is a small piece of their art, and their Adobe craftsmanship does all the rest.

I've loved Adobe products for decades, as I wrote in an earlier section. But for me, the fun of this job lies in the shoot itself. It's all about talking with people, crafting the image, hearing a great story and showing it back to them. I got into this business to tell human stories, and that's still what keeps me going, day after day.

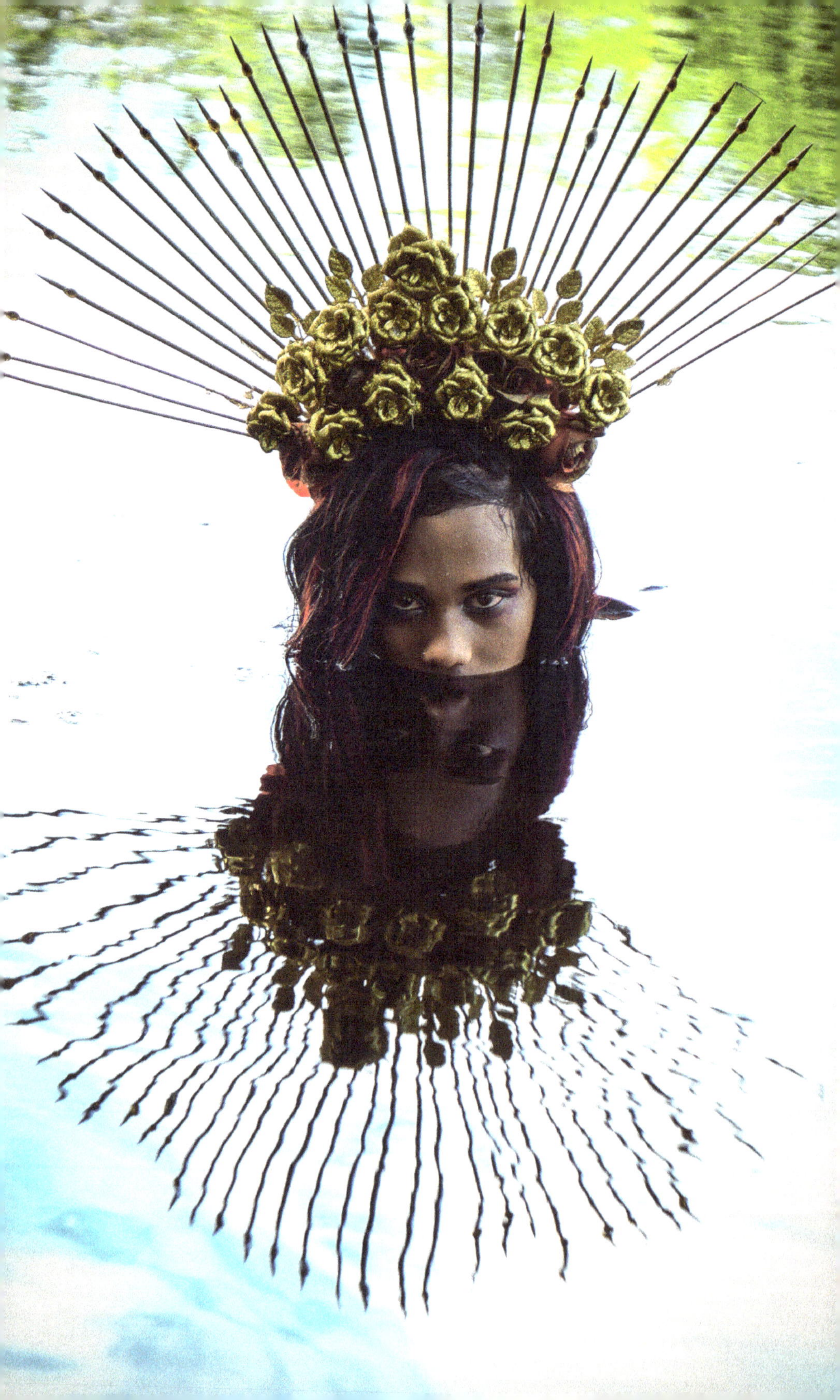

CHAPTER 11

PRIDE AND PROTEST IN GUYANA

"One has a moral responsibility to disobey unjust laws."

– Martin Luther King Jr.

In June 2019, one pre-dawn morning after an all-nighter of dancing and drinking, Joel Simpson walked up to his favorite breakfast joint in the Bourda Market, opened his mouth to order some food, and was knocked to the ground from behind. Six men jumped on him, kicking him and calling him names. A couple bystanders, one of them a police officer, tried to stop the men, but the gang was too strong—they swatted onlookers away and continued their assault, eventually dusting their hands of the situation and driving off in two separate cars. Joel was rushed to the hospital, but they discharged him shortly afterward. Bruises and cuts, but no broken bones.

Joel recognized the six guys. They had been eyeing him at a club earlier that night and threw beer on him and his friends.

Joel had decided to endure it. He wasn't surprised. It comes with the territory.

That territory is being gay in Guyana. Joel is the founder of the Society Against Sexual Orientation Discrimination (SASOD), a non-profit watchdog and advocacy organization that's been helping LGBTQ people in the small South American nation since 2003.

In lots of ways, Guyana is a unique country in the region. It's in South America but identifies as Caribbean. It's sitting on hefty oil reserves, but they were only discovered recently. Bordering on Venezuela, Brazil, Suriname and the Atlantic Ocean, it was never colonized by Spain, but rather by the Dutch and British before finally achieving independence in 1966. But some of the unfortunate parts of its history still linger. In the early 1800s, the British took over the region from the Dutch, and kept their laws banning gay sex, sodomy and cross-dressing. For numerous reasons, most of those laws are still on the books today. (The Caribbean Court of Justice knocked down its ban on cross-dressing in November 2018, which gives you an idea of how far the country still has to go.) Today, Guyana is the only country in South America to criminalize gay relationships.

I read about what happened to Joel with shock and horror, just a few days after returning home from my most recent assignment with Photographers Without Borders. I happened to meet Joel—in fact, SASOD was the organization with which I had been embedded for the last two weeks. This was a plot twist in my story that I never expected to write about.

DURING MY TIME IN Guyana, I didn't want to sleep. I anxiously waited for the sun to rise and shine on my door every morning, knowing that each day was a precious gift, unable to be repeated. In private, I wept for people most others don't know exist. I was eager to share my feelings with people I'd just met. Working alongside this diverse group, I learned to be completely free and open. I felt grateful for the fortune that had brought me here and longed to get lost in this new world.

But before arriving, despite my anticipation, I didn't know much about the history of gay pride, either in Guyana or internationally. I did a lot of research leading up to this trip, finding stories about men who were beaten and killed just for wanting to love someone of the same sex.

As it happened, I would be in the country during the 50th anniversary of the Stonewall Riots, the landmark event in 1969 that would give birth to the first Pride Parade in 1970. A half-century later, New York's police commissioner James O'Neill apologized on behalf of his department. But even until relatively recently, even in the United States, you could be married on Sunday and fired on Monday until the Supreme Court decided it was illegal for employers to fire or discriminate employees due to sexual orientation. We're fighting granular battles in North America, and I've been privileged to live in New York and Florida for most of my life, where such stories make up our national history. We take universal human rights and the joys of diversity for granted. In Guyana, that's far from the case.

Elsewhere in the Caribbean, other countries that have traditionally been plagued by homophobia have started Pride events in recent years, joining the ranks of the more than 150 official Pride celebrations that occur annually worldwide. Trinidad and Tobago, Barbados and even Jamaica (a country *TIME* magazine once called "the most homophobic place on Earth") have all staged annual parades, with activists declaring their place in society despite continual resistance. Cuba recently banned workplace discrimination based on sexual orientation and now offers free gender reassignment surgeries under its national health care system. Haiti's first LGBTQ rights organization, Kouraj, has brought well-deserved attention to the country's gay and trans community.

Guyana has fallen behind its neighbors. But that doesn't mean its LGBTQ population is going to simply accept the status quo.

ON SATURDAY, JUNE 1, 2019, the streets of Georgetown came alive with rainbow flags and vibrantly colored, carnival-styled costumes as their second annual Pride Parade took place. This event was indeed a sight to behold, with the parade starting at the capital's historic Independence Park and ending at the Square of the Revolution with revelers displaying their best dance moves to sounds of their favorite songs. About 200 people took to the streets, including some prominent faces from international governments to celebrate this joyous occasion. The parade closed with short speeches from members of the Guyana LGBTQ Coalition and the song "This is Me" from *The Greatest Showman* as people gathered, embraced each other and congratulated one another on another successful parade.

The parade marked the third day of Guyana's eight-day-long Pride festival. All told, the celebration included a panel discussion, an open mic, a symposium, party, a beauty pageant (dubbed the "Miss Diamond Infinity Pageant") and a queer film screening.

More than 100 members of Guyana Transgender United (GTU) worked alongside SASOD to plan the Pride events in Georgetown. Many transgender people in Guyana are rejected or harassed, so they frequently turn to sex work, which can be especially dangerous there.

My assignment for PWB was to meet some of these awe-inspiring people, and few locals stood out as much as my new friend Jasmin. She loved being photographed as much as I enjoyed photographing her. She struck me as an average 18-year-old girl in many ways: funny, inquisitive and easily hurt by social media bullies, but somehow wise beyond her years, and as resilient as the rest of her community.

Jasmin is a trans woman who first came to SASOD for assistance after getting assaulted in 2018. She later joined the team officially, working in their office, and is now part of the support staff on a temporary basis. "When I first came to SASOD, I was welcomed with open arms and treated like family," she told me. "They taught me that no matter who you are, you can be loved as equally as everyone else."

I have to admit I didn't know much about the trans community before embarking on this journey. (What little I did know, I learned from the excellent FX series *Pose*.) But Jasmin helped change all that, offering me a firsthand understanding of life in a minority group facing discrimination every day.

I also felt drawn to a woman named Quincy Gulliver, better known as Mrs. G. With a full figure and great sense of assurance, she leads Guyana Trans United with a warm, commanding presence. Although she was one of the first people I met in the country, I only got the chance to photograph her on my last day—in some ways, I feel this is the best way to shoot a portrait. I got the chance to speak with her multiple times to understand her struggles and successes, like how she led the way for the landmark cross-dressing lawsuit to fall in their favor. That was a law that had been in place since 1893.

Now, because of this woman and countless others who fought alongside her, a 125-year-old law was struck down. Freedom won.

AFTER I LEFT GUYANA, I read the article about Joel Simpson's attack with alarm and confusion. The fragility of their entire situation sharpened back into focus. Following the incident, which left him badly bruised and hospitalized, Joel took to social media to detail what had occurred. Local journalists picked up the story. News spread fast, and I was glad to see so many people support him publicly.

It was an undeniably cruel, violent homophobic assault. But Joel's commitment and leadership continue to challenge bigots in his country, even in the face of physical violence. It isn't theoretical: it's a literal fight between life and death.

"Being the victim of a hate crime in Pride month reinforced for me why Pride is so important," Joel later told me. The attack has only fueled his mission, giving him more ammunition to push government officials to enact stricter laws and enforcement against hate crimes.

"Pride is a protest," he said. "Pride is political. None of us are safe until all of us are safe. Our visibility is resistance and revolutionary, and that's what Pride is all about."

I'm in awe that Joel can move on so quickly—I wasn't even

there at the time, yet I feel shaken by his assault. I can't leave this story behind. Because of this trip, I am a different person. I've changed. And that ought to be something we all strive toward: mature people acknowledge when it's time to change, when old views become outdated or prejudices simply can't be upheld.

Most people reading this will remember when gay marriage became legal in the United States, after the Supreme Court sided with the right of all people to marry any man or woman they loved, rather than uphold rules from an ancient biblical text. That monumental shift happened in our lifetimes. The happiness that decision created is tangible: thousands of LGBTQ Americans are now living happier, more fulfilling, less stigmatized lives.

There is always work to be done. We all need to continually challenge ourselves. We need to learn more about other communities with compassion and curiosity. It's difficult to maintain old beliefs when faced with someone who challenges them. We should learn who we are and stay true to our core values, which ought to be, fundamentally, security and happiness for everyone. Empathy is paramount. It is not about believing some external judge is scrutinizing how we treat a complete stranger sitting next to us, but about how we act in that moment, how we can make the world a better place, even just a little, every single day. It's a challenge we must accept, or else we slide back into bubbles of comfortable assumptions and prejudice.

Get discomfited. Get scared. Start at the beginning again. If you think you know it all, find something you don't know much about. Open yourself up, and I promise, you'll end up learning something you won't regret.

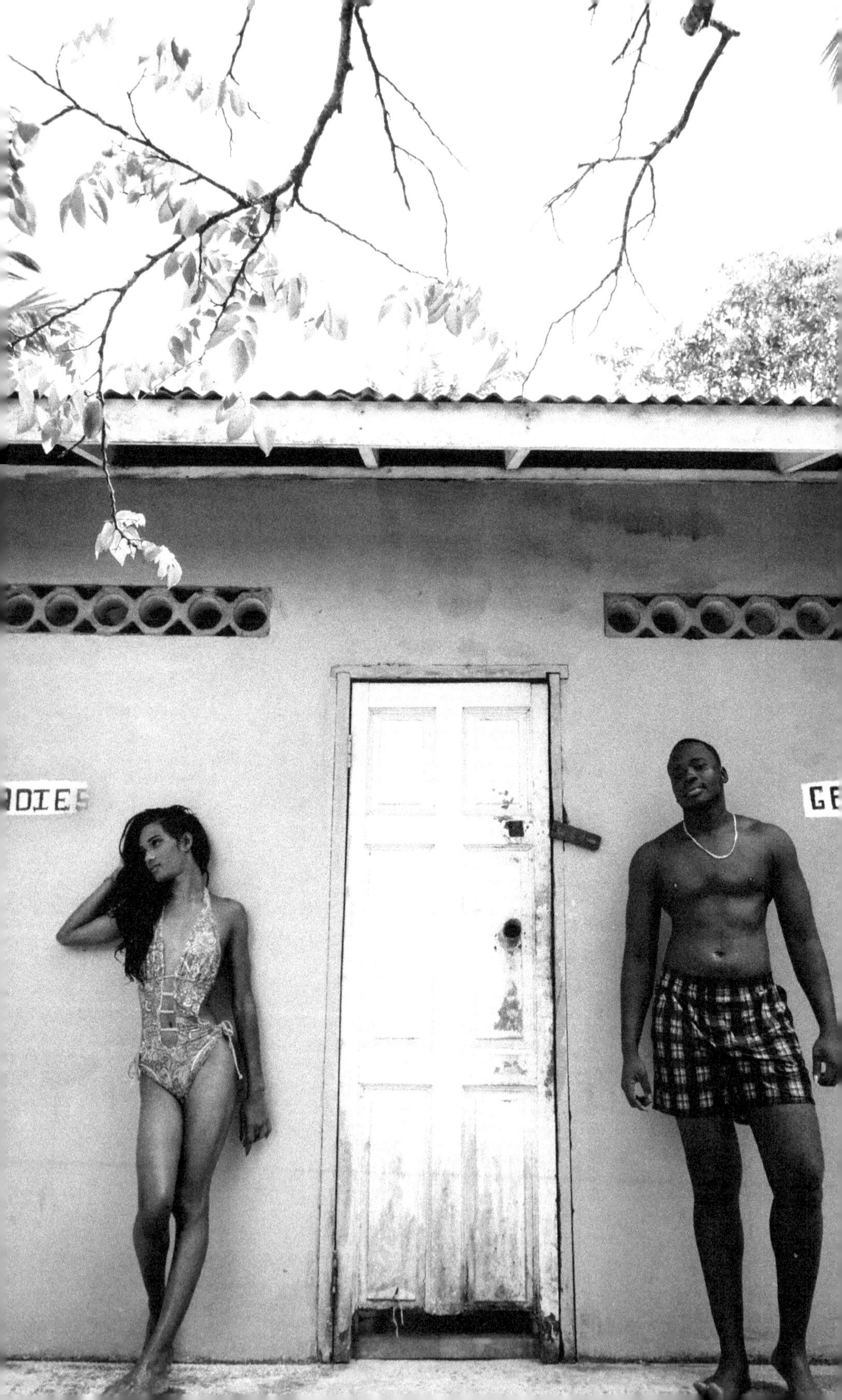
ADIES
GE

PHOTO TIP: THE JOY OF SHOOTING WEDDINGS

Over the last two decades, I've shot more than 500 weddings across the globe in places as far-flung as India, Aruba, Jamaica, the Dominican Republic, the Bahamas and across the United States. Wedding photography is one of my main sources of income, and a great complement to the life of a globetrotting travel photographer.

A lot of professional photographers supplement their passion projects (which often don't pay much, if at all) with more lucrative ones. Many go into commercial photography—shooting products for advertisements, things like that. Others prefer full-time portrait photography, which could include a lot of family portraits and corporate headshots.

I've done all that, but for me, wedding photography is ideal. It combines the skills I learned from photojournalism with my love of portraiture and fashion, all in a single, joyous moment. I love documenting the most important day in people's lives, when the room is filled with such high emotions: happiness, anxiety, sadness, elation. Everything and anything can happen on a wedding day.

I've been fortunate to have my wedding work featured in a

whole bunch of publications, including *Modern Bride*, *The Knot*, *Weddings Unveiled* and many more. I've picked up a few awards and accolades along the way. Now, I am in a fortunate position to be able to pick and choose which weddings I accept in a year, giving myself more time to get back to shooting the kinds of images that got me interested in photography so many years ago, including travel photography.

In building my business, I've trained and coached numerous associate photographers around the world who help me on these projects. In the spirit of this being an educational book, as well as one of storytelling, I wanted to offer a few tips on how to master the art of wedding photography.

1. **Build a relationship.** As a photographer, everything begins with trust. When your subjects trust you completely, they become more comfortable in front of the camera; this is what lets people shed their stiff, fake smiles and open up a little more. You can see the softness in their eyes and the emotion in their lips. They might even feel comfortable crying in front of you—one of my award-winning photographs is of a beautiful bride with a single tear streaking mascara down her cheek. This is the most critical step, and it's important to establish from day one. Without a solid foundation, the project will be much, much harder for everyone.

2. **Be constantly aware of lighting.** Unlike commercial photography, during a wedding (when you're a fly on the wall), you won't have a studio lighting setup. The lighting will change dramatically throughout the night. Toast-makers will not always stand in spotlights. Dancers move around. Not all tables will be lit evenly. It's important to be constantly vigilant about this and be prepared to nimbly adjust your aperture and shutter speed as necessary.
3. **Experiment.** It's important to have a checklist of shots that are "must haves"—portraits, close-ups of objects like the cake or rings, a dress shot, and so forth. But once you get your safe shots, you should stretch yourself. Not only does this help you discover more creative and unique shots (which is great for your portfolio and clients), but it also makes the job way more fun. You should love what you do, and keeping things fresh is critical to that. I always think to myself, "I'm not just shooting for the client—I'm also shooting for myself."
4. **Go above and beyond.** Shoot every subject to its full potential. Your clients will be far happier if you give them more than they asked for. That means looking at the same person, or the same building, from multiple angles. To find the whole story, you have to look at everything from different perspectives.

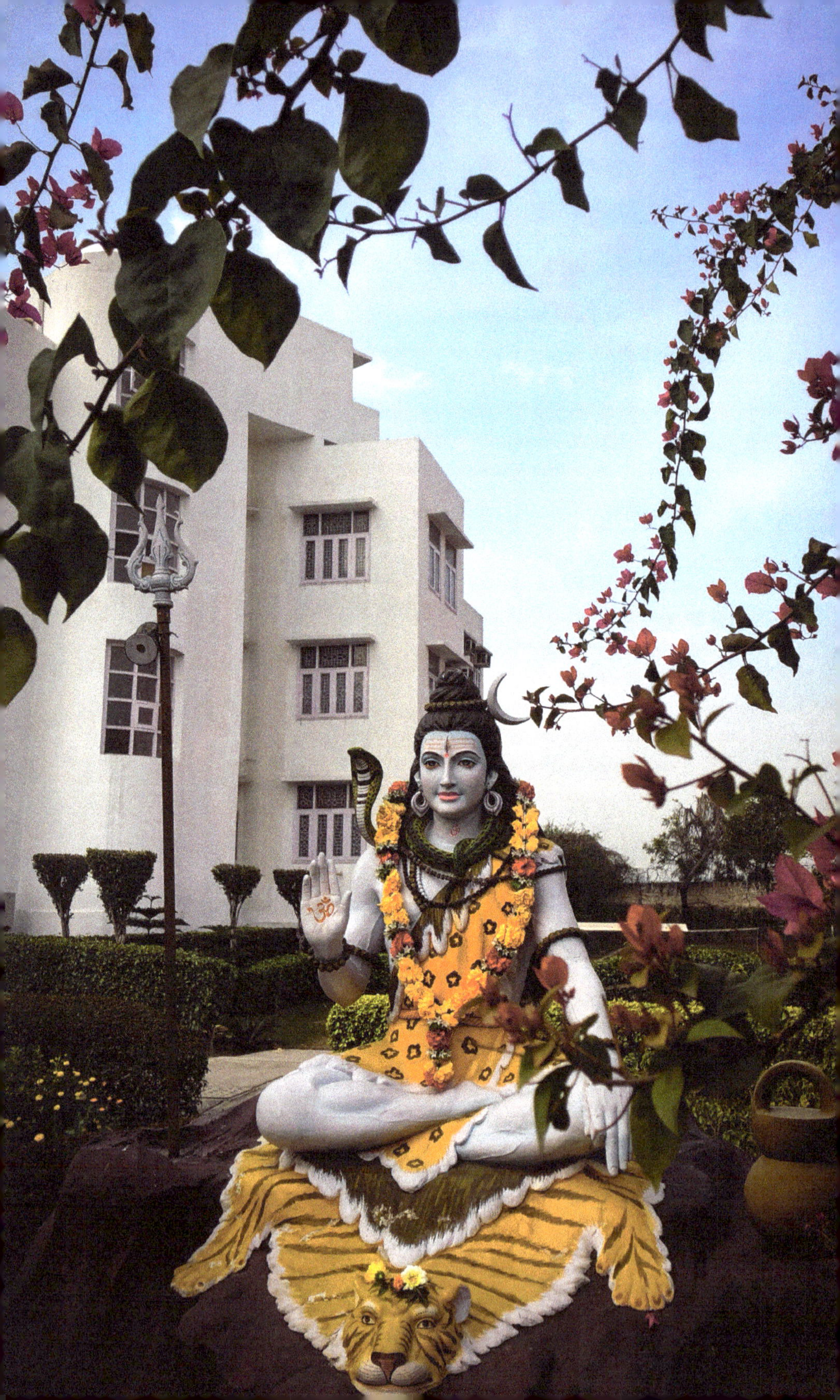

CHAPTER 12

GETTING HEALTHY IN DELHI

"The world is the great gymnasium where we come to make ourselves strong."
– Swami Vivekananda

After a photo assignment took me around Thailand and India for the better part of a month, I noticed that I'd perhaps eaten and drank a little too much at times. Add that to having an occasional cigarette (I know, I quit years ago!) and never seeming to get enough sleep, and the answer struck me as obvious: I needed a body reset.

I haven't always been kind to my body, especially in the year following 9/11; my job is also quite physical, and I've pulled my lower back several times during photo shoots. As a result, I've been interested in global health and wellness practices for a while now, and am always on the lookout for new, unique experiences. I started acupuncture a few years ago, got *intonga* stick massages in South Africa, indulged in daily Thai massages in Chiang Mai, visited hammams in Morocco, enjoyed the advantage of reflexology and tried cupping therapy a few times. I meditate on as many mornings as I can, which is invariably never enough. One thing I hadn't tried is Ayurveda, the 5,000-year-old system of medicine that's popular in India. Since I was in the country and had a few extra days, I decided to try it out.

I would have loved to spend the recommended two-week period at a clinic in the state of Kerala in the country's south, where Ayurveda is most well known. But I only had five extra days in Delhi after my mesmerizing trip to Bihar with Photographers Without Borders. So I decided to spend those extra days at a center called the White Lotus.

My days consisted of learning basic yoga poses (it was my first time), enjoying various kinds of massages, enduring hot medicated oil treatments, enjoying cleansing vegetarian meals and drinking lots of green tea. Believe it or not, after five days, I strolled out of there leaving my stress and anxiety behind—along with six needless pounds of fat.

Ayurveda—from the Sanskrit words *ayur*, meaning life, and *veda*, meaning knowledge; the phrase essentially means "to know life"—is one of the oldest forms of medicine, and seeks to treat problems in the mind, body and spirit using a holistic approach. It combines healthy eating and herbal remedies with exercise, meditation, breathing techniques and physical therapy. The goal is to let practitioners walk away with a stronger direction with regards to their diet and lifestyle, whether they were generally healthy before or not.

On my first day at the White Lotus, I was greeted by Dr. Amit Verma, who performed a quick examination and asked me some questions about my health and short-term goals for my visit. I explained that I'd spent the last few weeks riding around rural areas of Northern India on the back of a motorcycle carrying heavy photographic equipment. I hadn't been eating or sleeping properly, and wanted to relax, feel rejuvenated and maybe lose a few pounds. He gave me some advice about the benefits of vegan food, yoga and meditation, writing it all out for me as if it were a list of prescriptions. After a quick weigh-in, I was whisked away to my apartment-style room and began treatment within an hour.

Ritesh, the in-house yoga guru, had his hands full getting me started with yoga. It's something I've always wanted to try but could never really push myself into. At 50 years old, six-foot-five and a little overweight—not to mention uncoordinated and not a fan of the gym—I wasn't exactly a prime candidate for yoga. But all we did that first day was stretch, and Ritesh was patient, professional and exactly the kind of instructor I needed to get started. Part of the reason I never tried yoga before now was my fear of being in a room full of people who already knew everything. I was afraid of being embarrassed. But this was perfect for me to get introduced to yoga personally and without fear of judgment. When my first session ended, I said, "That's it? Awesome!"

My daily physical therapy consisted of various procedures that lasted roughly three hours in the late morning or early afternoon. The main procedures were called *nasya*, *shirodhara*, *abhyangam* and *patra panda sweda* (PPS). *Nasya* involves lubricating the delicate skin of the nasal passages and the eustachian tubes of the ears with a special herbal-infused oil. The cervical lymph, which is the stronghold of immunity in our ears, nose and throat, also benefits from this lubrication. *Shirodhara* is done by pouring warm medicated oil on the forehead in a sweeping motion to help relieve symptoms of anxiety, stress, fatigue and hypertension. This is also meant to help with sleep disorders. *Abhyangam* is essentially a full-body massage with plenty of warm oil, which has been pre-medicated with herbs for specific conditions. Two therapists perform the massage in a firm, synchronized manner. Finally, PPS focuses on the leaves of various plants that are fried with particular oils and other medicines, all of which have pharmacological and therapeutic properties for pain relief, inflammation and stiffness. The warm ingredients are wrapped in thin paper and patted firmly around the whole body. This was my favorite procedure.

All of these treatments—along with a balanced and healthy diet, stretching and rest—sure seemed to work for me. Will they cure a life-threatening disease? I'm not sure. But will they help relieve stress and reset your body in a comfortable way? Absolutely! The best part: the whole process helped prepare me for my more than 24-hour flight home. I've never felt so relaxed going to the airport, walking with newly found confidence.

And on the plane? I slept like a baby.

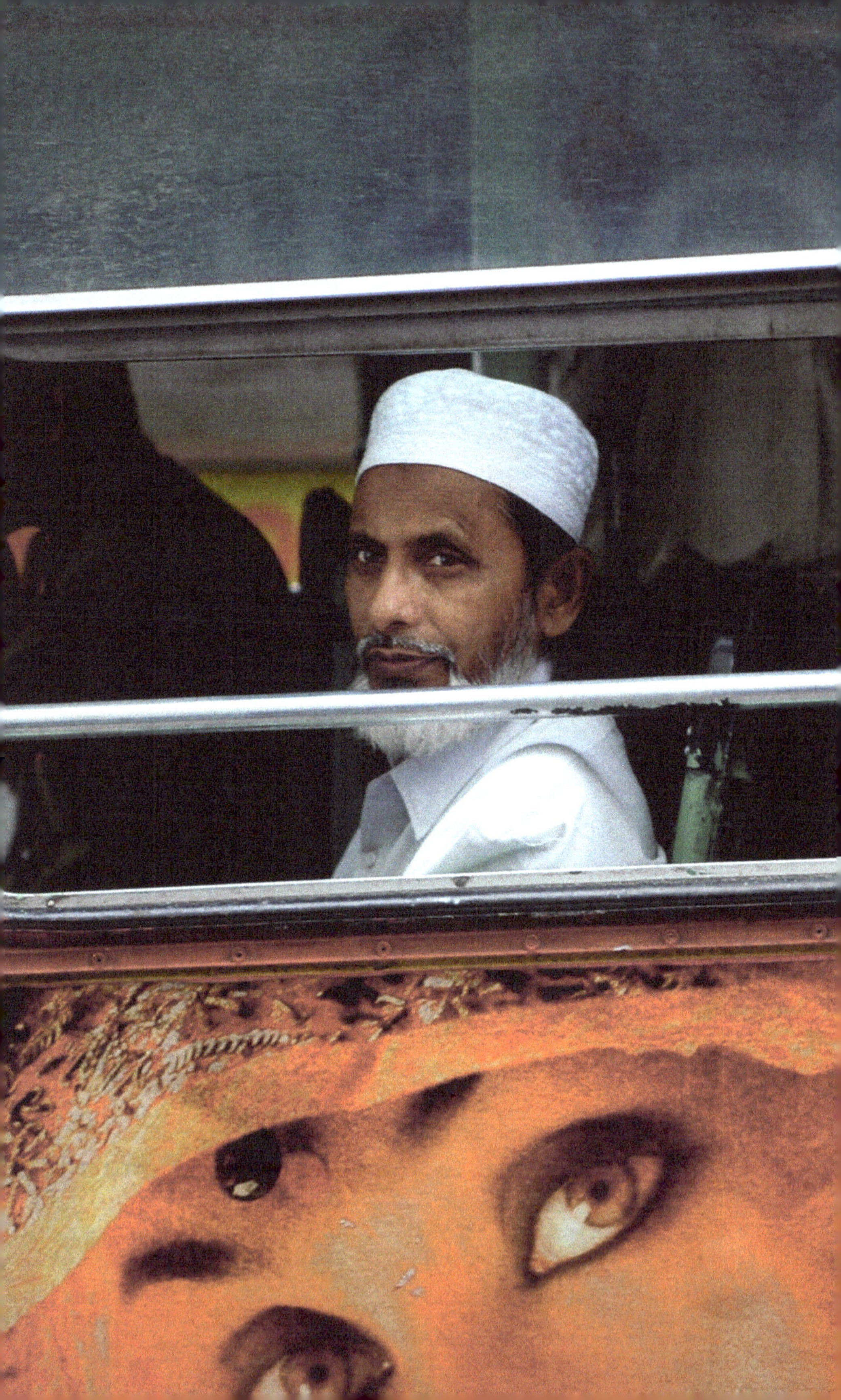

PHOTO TIP: DEALING WITH CRITICISM

A healthy body starts with a healthy mind. Everyone knows eating well and regular exercise are fundamental to a healthy lifestyle—but in addition to those physical treatments, mental health matters just as much.

On your journey, whatever it may be—as a photographer, an artist or even just a human being—you're going to encounter criticism. It's inevitable. Someone is going to tell you how to do something better, whether you've asked them to or not. Some people are better than others at accepting this criticism, but your first reaction shouldn't be to get angry at the person delivering it. Try listening instead.

This is painfully true in the photography community. Getting feedback on your photos is critical. The critique doesn't have to be professional: it can come from your friends, fellow photographers or even just strangers online. There are whole communities of people looking to connect with fellow photographers to shoot together and compare photos, learning and growing together.

Critiquing a photograph can be difficult, especially if you tend to follow your gut. You may simply like or dislike something and can't put it into words. Personally, I compare photography critiques to going to a movie: I either like it or I don't. Thumbs up, thumbs down. That's as good a starting point as any.

From there, you can ask yourself a few other questions. Does the image make you feel something? Does it tell a story? If you like one aspect of it, is there anything that feels distracting?

There are technical questions you can ask, too. Is the exposure correct? Would it look better at a different focal length? How is the composition? How balanced is it? What's happening in the background? Do all the colors work together? Does the photographer use different elements, like textures and shadows?

When I was a student at the Art Institute of Fort Lauderdale, every week, my fellow students and I would critique each other's work. I was always a little thin-skinned when it came to hearing negative comments on my photographs, but I didn't have a choice back then. In hindsight, I'm glad we engaged in those weekly critiques—they helped me learn both the craft of photography and the tastes of my peers. Art is subjective, after all, and no two people will love all the same things.

SINCE MY SCHOOL DAYS, I've entered different photographic competitions pretty regularly. One competition is attached to the annual Wedding and Portrait Photographers

International trade show, held every March in Las Vegas. I'd gone to the WPPI a few times before entering my own work in their competition, and whenever I attended as a mere attendee, I would take an entire day to just walk around the gallery rooms and study the winning images. I was always floored by the awesomeness of these pictures, the impact they had, all the immense talent and dedication it took to conceive, produce and present such beautiful artwork. I took the time to read the photographers' names and hometowns. There they all were, rooms upon rooms of photographs, all of which scored at least an 80 (out of 100) by multiple judges. These images were made by legends, some of them I considered personal heroes—people whose work I followed, even a few friends.

In 2013, I decided for the first time to pull my own entries together and mail them off overnight to the WPPI headquarters. The moment I walked out of the FedEx, self-doubt set in, and I spent the next month going back and forth about whether my images were really worth submitting. Maybe I sent the wrong choices. Maybe I wasn't good enough. I turned online for advice, and to read more about the competition. All the experts said how valuable it was to be present during the judging itself—to actually sit in on the process. Merely receiving a numerical grade wouldn't tell me anything, they advised. It was an invaluable experience to hear your work, and the works of others, being critiqued by a panel of world-renowned photographers.

In the end, I decided to take the plunge. The judging takes place before the trade show, so I flew to Las Vegas a few days earlier than usual. Then I went one step further and volunteered to be a print handler, giving me the opportunity to work in the "premiere room," where first-time entrants were judged—that's where several of my own images would end up. I would literally, basically in secret, be handing over my work to a panel of judges to eviscerate, laugh at—or maybe praise highly.

People will tell you that being in the audience for this kind of judgment is nerve-racking enough. There I was, standing in the literal spotlights, when I saw the first of several of my photos come to the forefront. This was one I debated heavily about entering—it was probably my least favorite. My heart was racing.

Here's how the scoring works: a panel of five judges rate the print, then you see the five numbers come up on the screen. The moderator calculates and announces the average score, and anything higher than an 80 is determined a winner. After debating the merits of my work, the judges gave their numbers, which flashed before me. Some were in the 80s. Others in the 70s. I can't imagine what my face looked like, if I was holding onto my poker face or starting to sweat profusely.

The moderator announced the final number: 79.

I was shocked. This was my least favorite image, so I figured I had this thing locked up. If this print scores a 79, then surely all of my others will be awarded! One judge challenged the score and argued for a re-vote. I fought hard to contain my glee. The judges did indeed take a re-vote—but even then, the score stayed at 79. I almost wished I could have stopped their argument, just called out from a few feet away to assure them, “No, really, 79 is perfectly fine with me!”

Throughout the day, more of my images passed through the halls. But my optimism waned.

One image received a 77: “Wrong paper choice.”

Another, 76: “I don’t get it.”

A third, 75: “Average,” “Needs more contrast,” “No detail in the blacks.”

Another, 74: “Below average.” That one stung.

Yes, it was incredibly difficult hearing this told basically to my face. But did the experience make me think I was a bad photographer? Of course not! Before this experience, I didn’t fully understand what these judges looked for. I made some wrong decisions in which images I submitted. Besides, I had at least one image worth a 79, so it wasn’t a problem with me—just with the particular images I submitted. And my clients—the people who paid me to take these photos of them—they all loved their photos. Ultimately, if they were happy, that’s what mattered most.

Near the very end of the day, after riding this emotional roller coaster, I knew I had one more photo waiting to be judged. “The Swing,” I’d called it. In it, a kissing couple is standing beneath a large, scraggly old tree before a forest. A single wooden swing hangs from the tree beside them. I'd edited the photo to resemble an old sepia photograph, with textured skies and delicate framing. The judges discussed it for a few moments—it was getting some good feedback. Then the moderator announced the final score: 81.

My knees got weak. I'd actually done it! The next day, as I entered the galleries, I was so overwhelmed by viewing these inspiring, emotional, funny and amazing photographs. Finally, I saw mine hanging there with the ribbon and seal of excellence, among the world's best wedding photographers.

I stared at my photo for a little while. It felt satisfying, but if I'm being honest, it didn't fully suppress my doubts. I kept wondering if I was on the right track. Maybe I *was* just average, and simply got lucky with this one.

Then I turned the corner and saw it. Another one of my photographs had made it through, having scored high enough to hang in a different category. It was total affirmation of my beliefs, my life goals. I felt fulfilled. It was an honor to see my hometown, Green Cove Springs, listed alongside entries from Los Angeles and New York City.

Despite my photographs that didn't make the cut, I knew I was on the right path. I was not just average. I could improve. And it took a leap of faith—putting myself in the spotlight before a panel of judges—for me to figure that out.

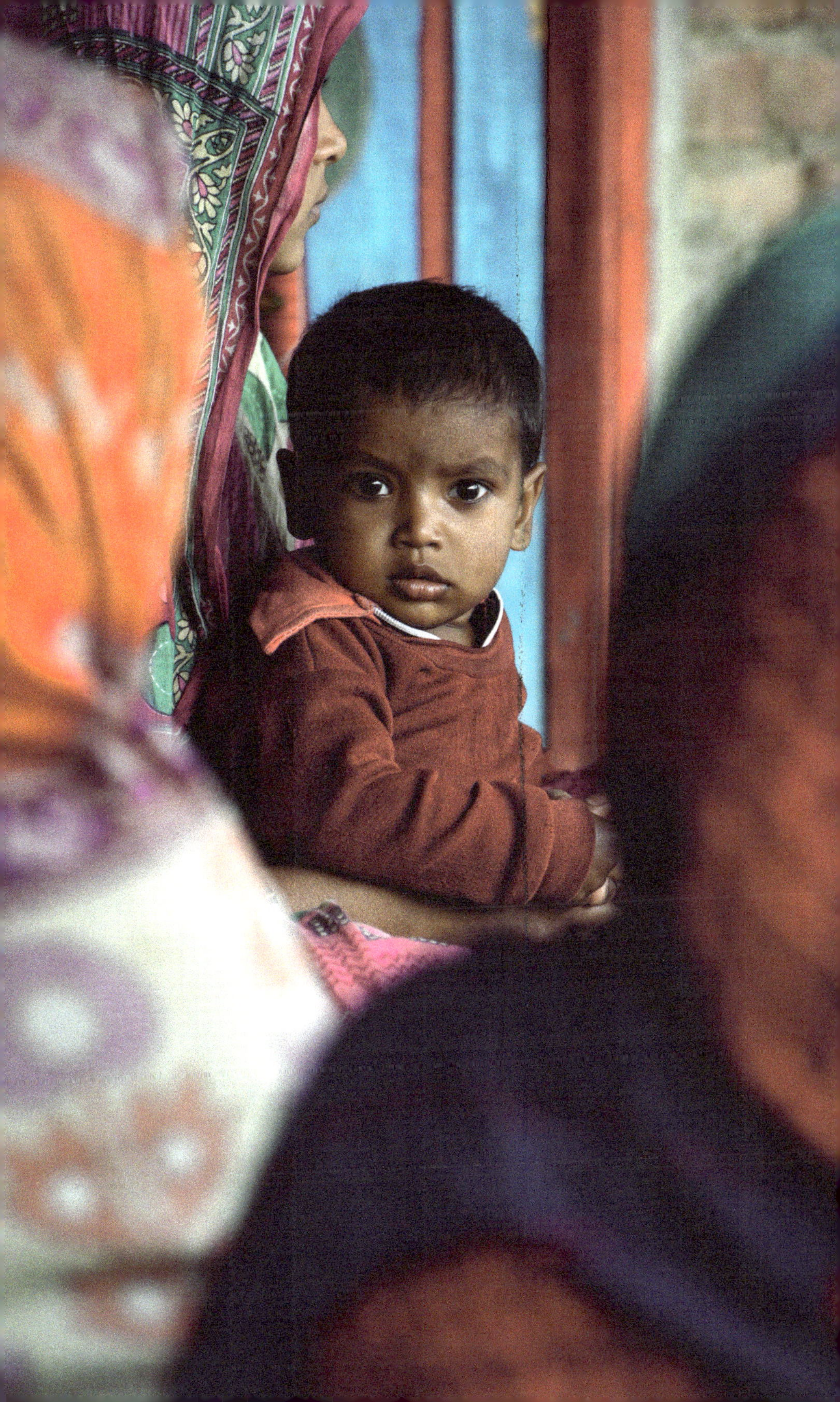

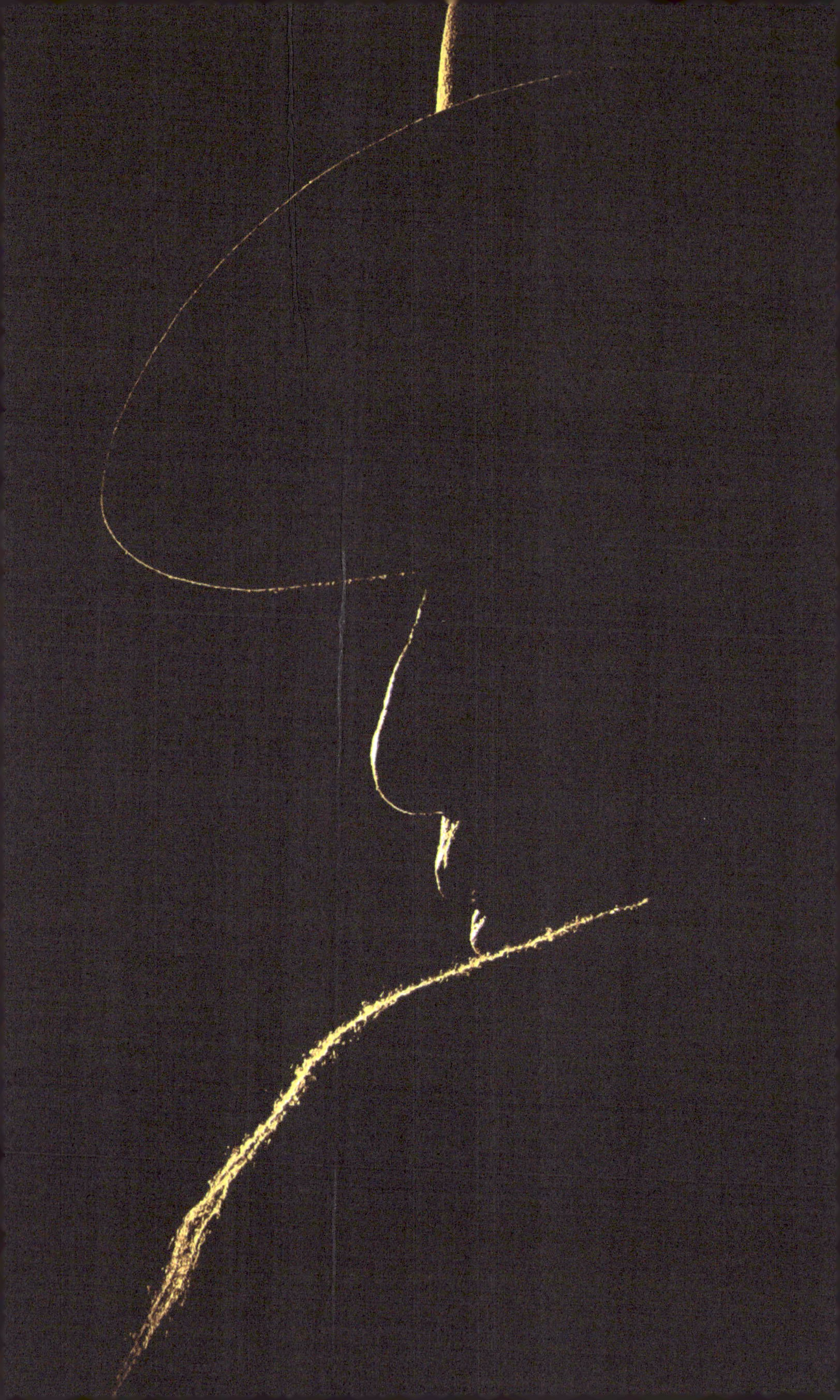

CHAPTER 13

WHY I TRAVEL

"Traveling: it leaves you speechless, then turns you into a storyteller."

– Ibn Battuta

Over a mountain, a sun begins to set and a moon climbs. I'm in a bustling city street or on a country road. Dark-skinned bodies shake and dance in a joyous parade. The nuclear power plant liquidator rests his head against his wife's shoulder, dreaming of what life together could have been, as the morning train heads north through Belarus.

Meanwhile, the photographer prepares himself for another adventure as his bus careens south, toward the unknown.

It is human impulse—the duty of the traveler—to absorb as much of a place as we can, to share that knowledge and spirit with the world, and to leave a little piece of ourselves behind.

Before each new trip, for me, a familiar emptiness comes back. It's a strong feeling, but also the lack of any feeling at all—a black hole, devoid of ambition, sucking me in. Daily routines exhaust me: the same streets, same faces, same choices to make.

To break free of this sameness, to express my freedom to choose a different path in life, is what keeps me going, even when I'm stuck at home. I ache for change.

I've been asked about my travels, often from people who don't travel as widely, more times than I can count:

"How can you just pick up and go?"

"Why are you going *there*, of all places?"

"When are you coming back?"

I cannot answer these questions straightforwardly. It's an odd thing about my travels: rarely have I chosen them; they often choose me. Whether it's the streets of New York and Mumbai, the beaches of Morocco and Brazil, the thrill of Chernobyl and Guyana—these places find me, they fall into my life. Every step is inevitable and brings us to where we are meant to be.

An old bed is sometimes the only friend I have. When the shadow of a window pane slips past me on the floor of a rented room, I know it is either time to rise or to make plans. A leopard that can see in the dark skulks through the night; a nun smiles up at a statue of Jesus Christ on Semana Santa. They are my witnesses. They're why I travel. Lifting a camera helps me focus on others and, in turn, learn about myself.

I shut the door behind me, and know I'll soon be there.

THERE HAS TO BE SO MUCH more than this. There is so much knowledge out there, so many cultures and traditions. We can shut our minds to the calling of adventure, but we cannot silence our hearts. I've learned to follow my heart whenever possible, even though it can be easy to ignore. Our minds bog us down with fears and anxieties, from the great existential threats of climate change and COVID-19 to the recent political tensions sparked by the death of George Floyd. Reflecting on my own life lessons and travels, I see so much human history forgotten: the Soviet mistakes in Chernobyl are being repeated during the coronavirus pandemic; the anti-racism movement that swept over Southern Africa seems to have only made modern-day Americans complacent with the status quo. Misconceptions about Cuba have ebbed progress made by Barack Obama; prejudice continues to divide the Western and Arab worlds; LGBTQ people are still fighting for the right to live like everyone else; HIV and AIDS continue to ravage Africa.

I'm writing this book in 2020, a pivotal time that I foolishly once believed was going to be "my year." I had assignments arranged in Bangladesh and Haiti, plus a speaking engagement in the Middle East. But my plans don't matter anymore. I'm housebound and restless, like everyone else. What fuels me in these moments, rather than experiences, is curiosity. This seems to be the dawn of a whole new era, and I'm listening closely to voices that describe a life vastly different from my own. That's what the world needs right about now: more people who discover who they are by listening to others.

The truth is, even at my age, I don't always know who I am. I'm exhausted by seeking validation and permission, trying to impress people. Yet I still do these things. I suffer hints of what could be a mid-life crisis, an existential dread. Travel used to help with that—but what about when we can't? Eventually, something has to change.

Listening to others is a good way to start. When I turn on the TV these days, I watch a global pandemic unfold and the death of an unknown hero mobilize a generation. I see a bitter election unfolding in the months ahead. I cannot help but wonder: Are we, as a people, too broken to fix?

All this makes me want to define my purpose, find myself. That means slowing down. Life is not always a race, where we have to speed up to keep up. It's more like photography: we have to slow down, open ourselves up to something new, and connect with the outside world in the serendipitous snap of a moment.

Life comes and goes if we don't focus on what we really want. But I know what I want—I want to be a donor and an investor in the world. I want to make more deposits than withdrawals. I want my words and actions to carry weight, not to be fleeting and inconsequential.

Travel allows me to establish myself in the world, to make something real, to manifest things. Traveling gives us more stories to tell. And marginalized people have the right to share their stories with the world as much as anyone—maybe even more so. Privileged people like myself can help with that. I believe I was not born in the USA just to sit in my backyard and barbecue chicken on weekends, but to use my advantages, my resources and abilities, to help those who don't have what I have. These are gifts to help others. Regardless of your passions, you must concentrate on what is important and what is real.

Don't be afraid of the road less traveled. Heck, any road at all will do. The person who leaves is not always the same person who comes back. I don't want to reach the end of my life and realize I'm the same person I was at 17. I want to evolve, to grow. I don't want to regret decisions I didn't make, dreams I didn't pursue, risks I didn't take.

Travel is soul fuel. It challenges you, scares you, inspires you. It forces you to reckon with yourself, your assumptions and emotions. Criticism always precedes greatness. Travel opens us up to spectacular things in the world. I want to plant one foot firmly at home with my loved ones, while the other foot sees as much of the world and what life has to offer as possible. *That* is the delicate balance worth striving for.

Reflecting on the resilience of the world around me, I realize we have to take responsibility for our past to truly know where we are going. These challenges are not new, but by honestly understanding them, we will be better prepared to achieve the real change our generation is capable of.

www.ingramcontent.com/pod-product-compliance
Ingram Content Group UK Ltd.
Pitfield, Milton Keynes, MK11 3LW, UK
UKHW062312290726
14090UKWH00018B/1028